Advance praise for
FIGHTING *for Our* FRIENDSHIPS

"If you're stalled or struggling in your friendships (and who isn't?), look no further. Sage and supportive, Danielle Bayard Jackson leads you to the more authentic, fulfilling friendships you've been searching for. Packed with revelatory tips and scripts, *Fighting for Our Friendships* is your essential guidebook to sustaining and strengthening your most precious relationships."

—Ellen Hendriksen, PhD, author of *How to Be Yourself: Quiet Your Inner Critic and Rise Above Social Anxiety*

"Danielle has unlocked the secrets to transforming your relationships from merely okay to truly remarkable: take stock, gain clarity, shed old patterns, and embrace fresh perspectives. All you need to revolutionize your connections awaits here for you in this pivotal guide."

—Elizabeth Cutler, cofounder of SoulCycle and Peoplehood

FIGHTING
for Our
FRIENDSHIPS

FIGHTING
for Our
FRIENDSHIPS

The Science and Art of
Conflict and Connection
in Women's Relationships

DANIELLE BAYARD JACKSON

hachette
BOOKS

NEW YORK

Hachette Go, an imprint of Hachette Books
Hachette Book Group
1290 Avenue of the Americas
New York, NY 10104
HachetteGo.com
Facebook.com/HachetteGo
Instagram.com/HachetteGo

First Edition: May 2024

Published by Hachette Go, an imprint of Hachette Book Group, Inc. The Hachette Go name and logo is a trademark of the Hachette Book Group.

The Hachette Speakers Bureau provides a wide range of authors for speaking events. To find out more, go to hachettespeakersbureau.com or email HachetteSpeakers@hbgusa.com.

Hachette Go books may be purchased in bulk for business, educational, or promotional use. For information, please contact your local bookseller or Hachette Book Group Special Markets Department at: special.markets@hbgusa.com.

The publisher is not responsible for websites (or their content) that are not owned by the publisher.

Library of Congress Control Number: 2024931062

ISBNs: 9780306830617 (hardcover); 9780306830631 (ebook)

Printed in the United States of America

LSC-C

Printing 1, 2024

To all the girls I've loved before

Contents

Part Three
LETTING GO AND STARTING AGAIN

Author's Note

The research I cited in this book was carefully selected from trusted organizations and individuals who are known for taking great care and responsibility in their studies. While no single study can speak truth for every individual, it can illuminate our understanding of how certain groups of women *typically* function under certain conditions. You'll also see alternating uses of the words "female" and "women." In the ever-evolving discourse around sex and gender, I work to include language that reflects the identity of the participants in the studies I reference and speaks to all those who are navigating this world as women. I hope that no matter the details of your womanhood journey, you'll find insights that support you in building healthy friendships.

I'd like to acknowledge the limitations of this research, and I hope that the studies I have chosen to share inform the decisions you make about how to develop and maintain resilient friendships.

And finally, in this book, you'll read stories from real women. In an effort to maintain the privacy of these women, I've altered identifying details and presented some stories as composites of multiple accounts.

Sharing these stories will help illustrate my points about conflict and reconciliation, and anonymizing these stories will prevent some women from getting calls from ex-best friends demanding to know: "Wait—is this story about *us*?!"

Because, let's face it: that would be awkward.

Introduction

I keep having this dream where I'm speaking onstage when a woman in the audience suddenly jumps up and screams, "Liar!"

Startled, I shield my eyes from the spotlight, search the crowd, and squint to find the face responsible for that disruption.

It's her.

My college best friend.

And she came to this event just to call "bull" on the whole thing.

This is always the point where I wake up feeling guilty and anxious. And I think I know why I keep having this dream...

My college best friend and I met during our sophomore year. We were around nineteen years old, trying to figure out that tricky stage between childhood and adulthood while bonding over our shared love of poetry and neo-soul music.

But a few years after graduation, something shifted.

Actually, it was more like a series of imperceptible shifts over time that took us in separate directions. It's kind of like when you go to the beach and set all your belongings down in a certain spot on the sand. You get into the ocean and begin to splash around, and after a while you turn your eyes to the shore to check on your things only to discover that they're yards away, because while you were floating, you drifted halfway down the beach.

The end of our friendship felt like that.

Somehow it dissolved into polite pleasantries covering unspoken grievances, and I realize now that I could've saved it if only I'd had the courage to say something. But talking about what was happening to us felt too awkward. Running away from those conversations shielded me from the possibilities of her calling me out on my stuff, and I didn't know how to sit in the hot seat.

1

It felt safer to let things fade into nothingness . . . and then unfollow her on Instagram.

Yet here I am, years later, writing a book about how to fight for our friendships. And I can't help but imagine her picking up this book and saying to herself, "Girl, *please.*"

The Danielle that *she* knew was unable to be vulnerable. She was stubborn and pushy and proud. And now, somehow, *that* girl's writing a book?

Surely, she must wonder how I got here.

The Journey to Friendship Coach

Becoming a friendship coach wasn't exactly on my vision board as a kid. It actually happened after a series of twists and turns in my career.

When I graduated from college, I became a high school teacher and eventually worked my way up to department chair. Between classes and after school, the girls in my class would come to me and vent about their friendship issues. I didn't realize it at the time, but I was unofficially coaching them through it. While "counselor" wasn't in my job description, I saw firsthand the way that their issues with belonging and connection were impacting everything else—their mood, their grades, and their confidence.

When I left the classroom a few years later to start my own public relations agency, I foolishly thought I was leaving that "teenage drama" behind. I was working with self-assured, high-achieving women, after all. I just *knew* that things would be different. But it didn't take long before I discovered that they, too, were privately struggling in their female friendships. Sure, these dynamic women had no shortage of friends, but they didn't feel seen and connected in those relationships.

While prepping her for a media interview, one particular client confided in me that she had no problem making friends, but struggled to keep them. She was so focused on her career that she put friendships on the back burner, and she didn't think she had the skill of turning her surface-level connections into something more.

Later that day, I went online and—out of curiosity—typed "friendship books" into the search bar. At the time, there were very few results...and most of them were for children.

I thought, *Is this how we see friendship? As something that young people will struggle with but that adults will have figured out?*

I reflected on the mountains of resources we have to help us be better wives, better lovers, better mothers, and better bosses. But what does the lack of resources for platonic relationships reveal about the way our culture prioritizes friendship? And what does it say about a woman who's having trouble in the one area of her life that we believe should come naturally?

That was the moment I decided to read everything I could get my hands on about women's friendship. I leveraged my background as an educator, became certified to coach, and set off to study what the latest research has to say about women's conflict, communication, and cooperation.

Over the next few years, I had conversations with therapists, evolutionary psychologists, linguists, neurologists, and anyone else who could help me better understand the unique complexities of women's relationships from their unique vantage point.

Then, I started the *Friend Forward* podcast to begin sharing what I was learning, and it wasn't long before women were sending me DMs to enlist my help with everything from how to make new female friends to how to tell a friend she's not included in her wedding party.

Soon, I was being hired to speak at sorority conferences, getting DMs from celebrities asking for friendship advice, and consulting with doctors on how to manage tensions on women-dominated teams. I was hired by the NFL to speak to some of the players' wives and girlfriends about how to manage loneliness while their partners were on the road, welcomed a series of national media interviews (and features in *Oprah Magazine!*), and even partnered with the popular app Bumble as its resident friendship expert.

Suddenly women in their early twenties up to their midforties were coming to me to share insights for their friendship struggles.

There was so much diversity among the women I was working with, and that's when it hit me:

Friendship is the great equalizer. It doesn't matter whether you're a college student or a middle-aged entrepreneur—we're *all* trying to figure out how to have better relationships with the women in our lives.

Fighting for Our Friendships is my attempt to share what the research has to say about what it takes for women to form (and keep) healthy friendships.

Because we are unique. Our challenges, our language, our priorities— it's different from the way a man might experience this world. And because of that, our friendships have a certain complexity.

When the research continues to show that women's friendships are more fragile (but deeper!) than men's friendships, it's time we unpack exactly what makes female friendship so "complicated." Because I've found that it doesn't have to be a mystery.

What to Expect

This book is divided into three parts.

Part 1

In Part 1 of *Fighting for Our Friendships*, we'll explore the mechanics of female friendship in an attempt to understand what brings us together... and what tears us apart.

We'll also look at the ways in which conflict aversion and relational aggression impact our friendships when things get tough. Read this section to get a big-picture view of this kind of unique relationship.

Part 2

Part 2 is a handbook filled with tips and scripts to help you navigate the nine most common conflicts that emerge between women. While it's important to take an aerial view of women's relationships, we also need to be equipped for the day-to-day business of friendship.

Read this section if you're ready to take action. You'll learn what to say and do in sticky situations, and how to reframe your perspective in current friendships that feel difficult.

You'll also learn the signs that the problem might be... you.

Part 3

The final part of this book will help prepare you to move forward after conflict. There will be times when you and a friend bounce back from a falling-out even stronger than before. Other times, a friendship has simply run its course. Part 3 will show you how to release these friendships with grace, and then how to position yourself to invite new connections into your life.

Building Your Friendship Library

While I made every effort to cover as much as I could, this book is not an encyclopedia. I hope that it's one of *many* books on your friendship bookshelf as you work to collect a range of resources to support you on this journey.

The research I referenced was from sources who are well respected and prolific in scope, but I must also acknowledge the inherent limitations of this work. Much of the content may feel most applicable to millennial women in the West, but there are lessons that will resonate with the hearts of women everywhere.

Your unique experiences will shape your journey through this book, and whenever possible, I encourage you to supplement this text with other readings that address your specific needs at a more granular level to holistically equip you to enjoy healthier friendships.

My Prayer for You

There were several points while writing this book where I had to take a step away because my heart was overwhelmed.

While I've made a career of getting into the details of how women can resolve conflict, it sometimes feels like just that—details. Because in every DM and email and social media post where women are soliciting my advice for yet another friend problem, sometimes I wish they'd just get to the heart of the matter:

In our quest to collect hacks and tips for every pressing friendship issue, we're only trying to answer the same two questions:

> *How can I find friends who will love me?*
> and
> *How can I freely express the love I have to give?*

At the end of the day, no matter what you do or where you're from, we all want the same things.

We want to give generously without wondering whether we'll be taken advantage of.

We want to be able to tell a friend she hurt us with the security of knowing that after we do, *she'll still be there.*

We want to bathe in the light of our beauty with women who delight in our radiance, instead of fearing that shining will make us a target.

We want to throw our head back and laugh with abandon among women who love the sound of our joy.

We want to rest in the love of other women without counting the ways they might betray us.

The details may differ, but our vision of fulfilling female friendship is often the same. Yet there's so much work to do before we can know that joy. How do we make public proclamations for the things we can't privately reconcile? Admitting the depth of our yearning feels like too great a risk. So, we protect ourselves.

We become "guys' girls" who hate their own kind *or* we save posts about red flags to outwit women with bad intentions *or* we measure our generosity to avoid extortion *or* pretend to want "low-maintenance" friendships to buffer the pain of getting less than we desire.

It's exhausting.

I'm ready for more. And I want more for you.

While I've made peace with where things stand with my ex-best friend, sometimes I wish I could get a do-over. How would things be different if I knew then what I know now?

I find myself working to recover some of that loss in the friendships I've made since then. I'm expressing my love more freely, accepting correction without offense, and confronting conflict with an open heart.

And my life feels so brand new.

As you read this book, I hope you recognize a bit of your own friendship history, and more important, I hope you get a taste of what is possible in your friendship future as you uncover answers to those two central questions:

> *How can I find friends who will love me?*
> *How can I freely express the love I have to give?*

Because in a world where women are often undervalued and underappreciated, we need exceptional connections with other women who make us feel safe, seen, and understood.

That's the vision I'm fighting for.

And I hope that you'll join me.

Part One

THE ART OF
FIGHTING

Chapter 1

Health, Wealth, and Sanity

The Power of Female Friendship

I checked the time on my phone—*2:45 p.m.*

In fifteen minutes, I was going to have to hear her voice and explain myself. It was a conversation I'd been dreading for weeks, but she noticed my increasing distance and demanded to know what was going on.

Taryn and I had been friends for a few years, but recently there had been a...shift. I noticed certain comments and behaviors that made me question her loyalty, and I wasn't sure whether I was overthinking things or there really was cause for concern. With every indecipherable comment, my vision of her grew blurry. I couldn't recognize the woman I had befriended a few years before.

To be clear, Taryn was my girl. She had nothing but love for me, so surely the weird vibes I was picking up on were just in my imagination.... Right? I thought I was hiding my confusion, but I'd begun to pull away and things had become tense. We had to address it.

I grabbed a blue marker and scribbled a loose outline of key points on my office whiteboard. Maybe building a script would keep me focused and make things less awkward. Less painful.

God, the irony of it all.

As a friendship coach, I spend hours each week sharing strategies with women to help them navigate challenging friendship issues. But lately, I'd been operating more from my head instead of my heart—it had been so long since I faced my own confusing crossroad.

After years of helping women plan for tough conversations (*How do I tell her I want space? Should I tell her that I think she's jealous? How do I tell her I'm outgrowing this friendship?*), I was facing my own crisis. And I was overwhelmed.

Shouldn't I be good at this? Or did I foolishly think that intellectualizing conflict would somehow buffer me from the drama and heartache that so often accompany tough friendship transitions?

At 2:55 p.m., I walked to the refrigerator and slung the door open, searching for something to calm my nerves. A shiny beer bottle glimmered on the bottom shelf, and I glanced at the kitchen clock to see whether I had enough time to drink it before our call without chugging it like some guy at a frat party.

No. I needed to feel my feelings, no matter how painful or awkward it would be.

I was spiraling.

So, at 2:59, I took a few sips of water, turned my chair to face my notes, and shut my eyes to whisper a quick prayer.

"God, help me. Please let this go well." I honestly didn't know whether we were about to have a gentle heart-to-heart to map a way back to each other or if things would get ugly, the call ending with a messy and regrettable finale.

Suddenly, it was time. I tapped her name on my phone and when the line began to ring, my heart pounded so wildly that I briefly considered hanging up.

So, this is how it ends, I thought. *An awkward phone call on a Saturday afternoon.*

Taryn and I talked for nearly two hours. Then, as if on cue, my husband came downstairs. He assessed the room, trying to get his bearings after a nap, and his eyes caught on the manic notes that lined the whiteboard.

"Hey . . . what's going on?"

I let out a deep sigh. "I just got off the phone with Taryn."

"Oh, wow. Are y'all good?"

"I mean, I think so." It was more of a question than a statement. There were tears and apologies and tension, and at the end of it I was still left wondering, *What now?*

He laughed to himself, apparently amused by the whole thing.

"Y'know, you would *never* see two guys in this situation. It's just not gonna be this...complicated."

As annoyed as I was by his smugness, *he was right.*

A few hours later, we went to bed, and I found myself scrolling social media, trying to ease the weight of my emotional exhaustion with videos of people reacting to the latest episode of a popular show where contestants get married without seeing each other. (Why are there so many seasons?!)

But I couldn't concentrate because my husband's comments kept echoing in my head.

Complicated.

I stopped midscroll and opened a new tab, mindlessly typing "complicated" into the search bar.

The definition popped onto the screen and for a moment, I stopped breathing:

Complicated (adj.): consisting of many interconnecting parts or elements; intricate.[1]

Yes. YES. By definition, female friendship *is* complicated.

When you mention female friendship in a room full of women, you'll either be met with starry-eyed squeals ("Yasssss, I love my girls!") or cautionary tales ("Be careful with women. They're nothing but drama and cattiness.")

The truth is, it's both. And telling only one side of the story fails to capture the range of humanity within this type of relationship. Whether you look at your friendship history with fondness or fury, you can likely recall times when women had your back *and* times when they let you down.

The research continues to show that women's friendships tend to be more intimate and emotional than men's friendships, and it's likely because we bring so many "intersecting parts" to the table. Whereas men may be more inclined to compartmentalize these relationships, we often expect to find loyalty, emotional support, and symmetry with the women in our lives. But these expectations are exactly what allow us to experience greater depth and connection in our friendships ... which comes with a greater capacity for disappointment and distress.

While our friendships can be invigorating, they're also really fragile. The connection is often strong,

> ... until she gets married and moves away.
> ... until she fails to show up during a critical time.
> ... until she becomes a chronic complainer, overwhelming you with her negativity.
> ... until you realize she hasn't been reciprocating.
> ... until she begins to make life choices that you simply can't support.

How do we get past "until"? How do we account for the pile of former friendships we've collected over time? How do we navigate seasons of conflict when the tectonic plates of our friendship begin to shift—sometimes ever so slightly, sometimes all at once?

Intuitively, we know that friendship is good for us. That's why we continue to enter into them excitedly, ready to reap the benefits of all they have to offer.

This book, then, is not just about relationships, but about wellness. Because when we have quality friendships, it leads to happier, *healthier* lives.[2]

Female Friendship as a Wellness Essential

In the longest-running happiness study by Harvard University,[3] researchers found that the factor that has the greatest impact on our overall life satisfaction and well-being isn't our income or our marital status—it's the *quality of our relationships*.

And when it comes to female friendship *specifically*? Let me tell you: it's next level.

Several studies suggest myriad physical, mental, and emotional benefits of being in the company of other women. One primary benefit is having lower cortisol (the stress hormone) levels[4] after seeking out female friends as a stress response, which leads to better heart health[5] and a decreased risk of dementia.[6]

Women who have strong bonds with other women also:

- Receive more emotional support[7]
- Have more career advancement and make more money[8] than women who don't have female-dominated circles
- Experience more satisfaction[9] in their romantic relationships
- Are better able to regulate their emotions.[10]

About 70 percent of our social network is same-sex (with most of our coed relationships being made up of family members).[11] The good news is that there's something powerful about having women in our social network. We need these friendships to serve as both a mirror and a model of who we are and what we can become. These friendships are at the center of our identity work.

It's important to be affirmed by those who know what it's like to navigate the world as a woman, providing the information and support we need to thrive.

Yet despite the power of these bonds, they sometimes don't get the respect that they deserve.

Female Friendship as Serious Business

I'd just finished a presentation at a business summit in Nashville, Tennessee, when two women followed me to the back of the room. My talk was filled with surprising research about how female entrepreneurs fare better when they have meaningful platonic relationships, and the audience seemed to have received it well.

"We loved your presentation. It's been our favorite one, so far," they whispered to me conspiratorially.

"Thank you so much, I appreciate that!"

"To be honest—" one of them began. She looked at her friend for permission to continue, and her friend nodded with encouragement.

"When I saw that there was a talk on female friendship in the program, I expected it to be...fluffy, or—I don't know—like 'girl power' and all that. I didn't expect it to be so...serious."

I wasn't surprised to hear that.

A few years earlier when I first decided I wanted to pivot and become a friendship educator, I wasn't exactly saying it loud and proud. I was actually a little embarrassed. When I was a high school teacher, people called me a "hero." As a publicist, they called me a "badass." But as a friendship coach? Yeah, it wasn't exactly cool.

I remember the day I announced it to the monthly book club I was a part of at the time. The group was made up of lawyers, marketing VPs, and entrepreneurs who'd sold *multiple* companies to Google.

We met in a fancy high-rise in downtown Tampa, and each meeting began with us going around the circle and sharing a life update. On this particular day, I was hesitant to let them know about my potential career change—these were very serious women, after all.

When it was my turn, I made the announcement: "So, I think I'm gonna be a friendship coach..." I feigned confidence in hopes that it would mask the internal cringing.

I scanned the room, desperately studying their microexpressions to detect any condescension or disapproval. Some of the women lifted their eyebrows in surprise, asking questions and offering heartfelt congratulations.

But there was one woman.

She quickly cut her eyes to someone across the room with a look that said, *Is she serious?* and then they both smirked. It all happened so fast that if you blinked, you would've missed it.

"Wow," she spoke up. "That's so...*cute*."

Cute. As if I'd just declared that I was going to become a professional baby-hugger.

I pretended that I didn't hear it and moved forward with explaining exactly what I'd be doing. Most of the women were supportive; others were skeptical.

When we were younger, we often saw female friendship represented in extremes: there were images of girls braiding one another's hair at a slumber party and the other girls who were calling names and getting into catfights. Then, as we got older, some of us began reducing friendship to a recreational pastime, something we'll get to when we're not busy with work or children.

It doesn't help that the study of friendship itself is sometimes viewed as "women's work," and not met with the same gravitas of other disciplines.

In *The Social Sex: A History of Female Friendship*,[12] feminist author and historian Marilyn Yalom identified four key ingredients of women's friendships: affection, self-revelation, physical contact, and interdependence. Since our society views most of those qualities as inherently feminine, friendship itself is sometimes dismissed as a female notion—a go-to staple of a patriarchal society that consistently frames women's interests as frivolous.

And in the academic world, friendship's considered a "soft science," a label that emerged to differentiate between male- and female-dominated STEM disciplines. Those who have committed their careers to studying friendship have been met with skepticism and condescension. A focus on *female* friendship, then, seems especially ridiculous.

But things are shifting. Women have always spoken to the power of female friendship with intellectualism and seriousness, and that discourse is getting more of the spotlight as men are less able to gatekeep these spaces, determining which research gets funded and whose stories get shared.

With more literature, media, and resources on the subject, we can better understand the complexities and value of women's friendship from myriad angles.

And while much of this work highlights the wonderful benefits of women's friendships, it explains the dark side too.

Guys' Girls, Girls' Girls, and the Dark Side of Female Friendship

There are many reasons that some women swear off female friendship. Whether their apprehension's rooted in serious friendship trauma, a lack of healthy modeling, or a belief that they just don't speak the language, it can keep them from enjoying the positive aspects of all female friendship has to offer.

Dr. Sahar Martinez is a therapist who specializes in generational and gender-related trauma. She explains why some women might avoid relationships with other women:

"In my late twenties and early thirties, I felt very traumatized in my own female friendships. I think a lot of friendship trauma comes from a combination of a lack of boundaries and a lack of self-worth. We give more than we're comfortable putting in, and when we don't get that in return because we haven't voiced our needs, it's painful."

She says that many women think that to end the cycle, they need to make changes externally (e.g., "I'm not going to become friends with women"), but the only way is to break the cycle internally.

"There's research that shows that women suffer from stress twice as much as men do. And so we're functioning from a baseline of stress; there *is* female-to-female victimization and emotional violence in friendship. That happens and that's real. But our feelings belong only to us."

Dr. Martinez says that women with these issues should ask themselves whether they want to stay in a place where they don't allow new friendships.

"We desire connection, so if there's hurt that's getting in the way, there's some healing to do. Healing is not dismissing the bad things that happened to you but accepting that the bad things happened and choosing to move forward."

Shena Lashey is a trauma therapist, attachment specialist, and host of the popular podcast *Black Girls Heal*.[13] She explains how women sometimes form this aversion:

"Typically, when women come to that place, they've gone through distrust and wounding, so naturally they go through a period of swearing [other women] off. If you're meeting people who want to be your friend, and you're shut down, how are you going to be able to meaningfully connect with them? You'll have to step out of that place of fear of rejection or abandonment."

And still, there are some women who believe they're simply too different to actually connect with other women. To avoid feeling confused and left out, they avoid the female-female dynamic altogether.

One of the most popular episodes of my podcast, *Friend Forward*, was one that focused on guys' girls and the reasons they prefer the company of men to women. Several women sent audio messages explaining why they currently (or formerly) viewed male friendship as preferable, and the top four reasons they offered were:

1. "Women are catty and competitive."
2. "I can't be myself around women."
3. "Women are too emotional."
4. "I have stereotypical male interests."

Whether it's cattiness, a lack of compatibility, or an uncomfortable reckoning with our own womanhood, there are ideas we hold of female friendship itself that directly impact our willingness to engage with it.

I spoke with a woman named Abby who shared her experience in more detail.

As a competitive swimmer in high school, she described the "girl team culture" as one filled with gossip and criticism; she felt unsafe because she never knew when she'd be the next victim.

"I constantly felt criticized—about my appearance, my mannerisms. And since then, I've always felt more comfortable with guys. Probably because I feel less scared that I'll be judged. I'm not thinking so much about how I'll come off...I can be more myself.

"With guys, I can also speak up if I disagree with something. With women, it's like a minefield. I don't know their touchy spots...and with guys, I feel less concerned about my appearance because they either don't notice or don't care, and our conversation's more about our shared interests. With women, the conversation tends to gravitate toward other women."

She was quick to clarify that this didn't always include gossip, but just a general tendency toward speaking about the details of others' lives—an interest she doesn't share. (And mounting research[14] confirms this, so Abby's observations are spot on.)

Abby also grew up with a lot of siblings, living with both sisters and brothers. "The women in my family are strong and opinionated, which I can appreciate, but I've always felt [more at home] with my brothers." She says that guys might start conversations by asking what she's into or about projects she's working on, compared to women who may want to know more personal things.

Abby *does* have female friends who she loves and appreciates, but there was a difference in how those friendships formed.

"Those friendships developed slower. We're bonding through what we have in common (which might not be much at first). And once we're friends long enough, there's safety for me [to be more myself]. And maybe those friendships take longer to form because...I have more hesitation."

Abby's first experience with women was with her mother and sisters, and it influenced how she related to the girls on her swim team. The experience there impacted how she showed up to female friendships as an adult, and now, how she'll relate to her own daughter.

This doesn't surprise Dr. Martinez, who says that evaluating our current attitude toward female friendship requires us to look at the models we had from the beginning.

"When we do the work around generational healing, we look at those relationships, and see how they impact us. Because a lot of times, our female friendships reflect the other female relationships we've seen throughout our lifetime."

I'm so thankful to have a mother who always encouraged me on my friendship journey.

Driven by the wisdom of *her* mother, Mae Fannie, who preached that "it's just nice to be nice," my mom always pushed me to connect kindly with other women in my life. She coordinated slumber parties for my birthday and stepped in during my teenage years when she sensed drama with other girls. She hyped me up when I didn't have the confidence to approach new friends in high school, and she held an intervention between me and two girls at church who were determined to make me miserable.

When she wasn't around, I faltered. Over the course of my friendships, I've been bossy and demanding, weak and insecure. I've been a "mean girl" and a pushover, a chameleon, and a know-it-all.

I also struggled to find my way among other girls who delighted in me as a target. I was nearly jumped in the bathroom in the sixth grade when a girl confronted me about "looking at her man" (the "man" in question was thirteen), and teased by a few "popular girls" during ninth grade for my hair and nose.

Through it all, my goal stayed the same:

I wanted a circle of friends who loved me. And I wanted to be able to love them back.

But all my "stuff" kept getting in the way.

And it helps to have the guidance of another woman figure to help us through.

Without healthy models of female friendship, we might become frightened by the idea of befriending other women, seeking refuge and companionship in circles dominated by men.

But when it comes to reconciling the divide between girls' girls and guys' girls, it can be a tall task.

Dr. Hannah Bradshaw is an assistant professor in the Department of Psychology at Washington & Jefferson College. Her research program draws from an evolutionary theoretical framework to explore such subjects as women's social relationships.

One of her recent studies explores the ways women's friendship preferences (specifically, women who prefer the company of men) impacts the way they view (and are viewed by) other women.

In general, in the research that I've done—these women [self-described "guys' girls"]—don't report being competitive *themselves* with other women, but they say that other women are mean to *them*.

It's kind of like this cycle. It starts right around when puberty hits. Maybe if you're young and you have issues socializing with other girls—because let's be honest, they can be very catty and mean to each other—you'll experience these kinds of issues. Maybe you're more likely to experience [this tension and conflict] if you enter puberty earlier, because people gossip about you. Girls especially, because boys are like "Oh you have boobs! This is exciting!" So other women are mean to you, or you have issues with the complex socialization process or the communication process between women, so you decide to be friends with the guys.

Dr. Bradshaw's research found that the relationship between "guys' girls" and "girls' girls" is bidirectional: Women who report experiencing hostility from other women seek the refuge of men, but their being in the company of men is what makes other women dislike them. And the cycle continues.

Here's what blows my mind:

One of the most surprisingly common issues that women bring to me as a friendship coach is a secret desire to create meaningful relationships with women *despite* having an aversion toward them. They share the painful experiences they've had with other women, and then express a hunger to still be loved by and connected to them.

As a coach, I am not equipped to help them make sense of past trauma the way a therapist might, but together we design strategies for them to actively position themselves to invite more female connection into their lives. We talk about the ways in which their anticipation of rejection and betrayal may impact the way they engage and experience other women. Then, we figure out how best to achieve their goals of creating new healthy female friendships—because the very source of their heartache is also the source of their healing.

Whether we're girls' girls or guys' girls, there's no denying that while women's friendships are deeper than men's, they're also more fragile.

Between a lack of supportive resources, a growing list of arbitrary and seemingly unknowable "girl codes," and poor models of female-to-female conflict resolution, we're in a situation that leaves many of our closest friendships ripe for dissolution.

Dr. Joyce Benenson is a professor of psychology and author of the book *Warriors and Worriers: The Survival of the Sexes.*[15] She's also conducted several studies about conflict, cooperation, and status in women's intrasex relationships. Her prolific body of research has found that—compared to men—women extend less leniency, have less resilience, and perceive more violations in their friendships.

Does this mean that many of our friendships are ending prematurely? If so, are we not accessing the fullness of all that these relationships offer? Is our fragility keeping us from experiencing the kind of platonic intimacy we crave?

Learning how to persevere during conflict will help us salvage (and deepen) ties with the women in our lives.

And that has the potential to change . . . well, *everything*.

Female Friendship as an Act of Resistance

Dr. Cori Wong is a feminist philosopher, writer, educator, and consultant whose TEDx Talk on feminist friendship[16] rocked my world. In it, she explains the bigger picture, drawing a connection between the significance of having authentic connections across differences in our personal friendships and the collective liberation that awaits us as we learn how to get it right:

> Feminist friendship is an inherently political practice of developing relationships marked by intimate bonds of understanding, care, and support that help us know how to show up for each other better across our differences. We can't really demonstrate our care or be in solidarity with one another if we don't know what we need from each other. And we won't know what we need from each other or what support really looks like if we don't understand each other's experiences.

> Dr. Wong argues that the nature of oppressive systems is to separate us, so the ability and willingness to connect across our differences is more than a solution to interpersonal conflict—it's an act of resistance to oppressive systems.

> The key piece that gets in the way is developing our personal capacity to even have a dialogue, to listen and understand. The ultimate goal is to be able to show up with solidarity and support, but we just can't jump there without having that foundation of care and understanding first.

Speaking with Dr. Wong helped me see the power and scope of this work. Learning how to fight for your friendships is about so much more than creating platonic relationships for your personal satisfaction. It's the key to collective liberation.

And I'm here for it.

But before we can learn how to keep our friendships from falling apart, we have to understand the magic and mechanics of exactly what brings us together.

Chapter 1 Questions

1. Describe your relationship with your primary female caregiver while growing up. Do you see connections between that relationship and the way that you relate to your female peers today?
2. Are there women who would point to a relationship with you as a positive highlight in their friendship history? Are there women who could name you as a villain in their friendship history?
3. Which movies, books, or real-life examples do you hold as ideal models of female friendship?

Chapter 2 Preview Question:

What does it take for you to feel close to another woman?

Chapter 2

How We Come Together
(and Why We Fall Apart)

The Three Affinities of Female Friendship

The year 2013 was a rough one for me.

I was suffering from major burnout as the academic chair at a high school in one of the country's largest counties, and my hair literally began falling out from the stress. I was also still reeling from a painful breakup, but worked hard to look like the picture of professionalism each day at school.

The premiere of MTV's *Girl Code* was a welcome distraction to my all-consuming struggle.

Girl Code was a show that featured women comedians giving their (oftentimes problematic) takes on all things womanhood. I'm not ashamed to admit that I learned a lot about periods, drinking, roommates, and makeup by watching this show. No—actually, I learned a lot about what *other* women thought about those things.

Esther Ku, a comedian who appeared on the show in its earlier years, validated my feelings.

"It's been years and I still come across a lot of girls who appreciated the advice and tell me that they loved the show."

Maybe it was such a hit because it took a humorous approach to outlining all the unspoken laws of being a woman. And while it was meant to be lighthearted, it also highlighted an unsettling truth: as women, *we've got a lot of rules.*

The laws for female friendship seemed to be especially extensive, as they govern everything from phrases you're supposed to avoid to gestures you're supposed to extend.

Navigating relationships with other women can feel like a land mine, knowing that, at any moment, you may turn someone off, hurt her feelings, or cross the line.

As a high school teacher, I looked on as some of the girls in my class tried their best to figure it out. They learned through trial and error. I saw what happened as they broke and honored these codes, losing and making friends in the process.

It was common for one of them to come to me after class, requesting to be reassigned to a new group because somehow—overnight, it seems— she made a misstep, and now she's getting the cold shoulder.

She broke a law she didn't even know existed, and everything (silently) changed. And this was a frequent occurrence in my classroom—my seating charts had the pencil eraser marks to prove it. These teenagers were learning how to relate to other girls. They had no idea that these experiences would shape how they formed and navigated friendships later in life as grown women.

Years after I left the classroom, I saw the same hurt and confusion expressed by grown women I worked with as a coach. They were either sharing disappointment over a friend who failed to show up for them in some way, or they were on the receiving end, expressing confusion over getting "phased out" by a friend (presumably over failing to meet some silent expectation).

As client after client sat across from me and gave accounts of their friendship conflicts, it was common for them to explain that their friends were doing something that was "obviously not okay." The irony: it was obvious only to them, and in most cases, the friends they were complaining about were often unaware of their missteps.

Wouldn't it be so much easier if we all shared one universal Google Doc listing our friendship dos and don'ts so we were on all the same (literal) page about what constitutes an offense?

The *language* to explain what's happening eludes us—but we know it when we see it.

And this doesn't just happen during the tough times in friendship. There are inexplicable moments during the good times as well.

Why is it that one show of support can move a woman up the ranks, from "acquaintance" to "bestie"? How do we explain a strong connection with a new friend who we suddenly feel we've known for years? Why is it that we like some women more after they share a secret with us?

How do we make sense of the magic that brings us together?

And how do we understand the mechanics of what tears us apart?

The Mechanics of Female Friendship

While studying the research on women's communication, cooperation, and conflict, I noticed something. When learning about these bonds through a neurological, sociological, or psychological lens, the same themes continue to emerge.

There seem to be three central principles that bond us together: **symmetry, secrecy, and support**.

I call them the *Three Affinities of Female Friendship.*

Once you understand their dynamics, you'll:

- Have language to describe why you and a friend have been "feeling off"
- Understand how to stay connected to friends during changing life seasons
- Be able to better explain the gap between what you need and what you're getting

And you'll generally gain a better overall understanding of *how female friendship actually works.*

When two women are operating in alignment with these "tendencies," they feel connected, secure, and supported.

But when there is a perceived violation in any of these three areas, there's tension. And while that tension doesn't necessarily mean the friendship is doomed (though some are!), it often signals that recalibration is necessary to get back on track.

The challenge is to find balance and shared understanding within each of the Three Affinities with our friends to keep the relationship going.

While no single framework can apply to every human being at all times, there's mounting research that shows these are things women *tend* to lean in to when they come together. Depending on our individual needs, insecurities, and expectations, one principle might be more relevant than others and fluctuate throughout the course of our friendships.

Using the Three Affinities as a touchstone can help you during seasons of conflict in your female friendships when you're trying to make sense of the shifts that are happening. They offer a starting point for figuring out how to enhance your connections with other women.

Without it, you'll continue to be burdened by the weight of an ever-growing list of arbitrary "girl codes," and pointing to your fatigue and frustration as evidence that female friendship is difficult.

But it all starts with gaining a better understanding of the mechanics.

Affinity 1: Symmetry

The first way that women bond with each other is by assessing and establishing symmetry. This can show up in a few different ways, including feelings of **sameness**, **equality**, and **reciprocity**.

Let's look first at feelings of sameness.

"I can't relate to her anymore."

When it comes to feelings of sameness, women have a greater tendency then men to associate with those they believe to be similar to them. While homophily (the sociological concept of associating with people who are like you) is a key ingredient for any friendship, women tend to prioritize it more than men do in their friendships.

Research[17] finds that *perceived* similarity makes us more inclined to trust another person—especially in the beginning of a relationship. This means that we don't have to actually be the same, but as long as we *feel* that we are, that's what matters.

Sameness does not necessarily determine whether we can be friends, but perceived similarity will determine the degree to which we feel close.

And according to a large friendship research study by Dr. Anna Machin,[18] the areas where we want to feel sameness matter. She finds that best friendships for women were strongly predicted by the degree of similarity in education, disposition, dependability, humor, and the number of shared activities.

In an essay, Deborah Tannen[19]—a sociolinguist who focuses on gender differences in language—explains how sisters relate to one another. Since so many women view their closest friends as sisters, much of the insights are transferable to close female friendships. In the essay, Tannen explains that sisters often attribute their level of closeness to a high degree of similarity; when making a case for why they're not close, they'll often point to how different they are. And when sisters are close but different, they mention their closeness *in spite of* their differences.

Each woman gets to determine where sameness matters to her.

For many women of color, this includes having friends of the same race to affirm this aspect of their identity.

Dr. Seanna Leath, an assistant professor in the Psychological and Brain Sciences Department at Washington University in St. Louis, has led studies that center on the need for these friendships.

"[Students] were in these predominately white higher ed contexts where there were not a lot of other women like them and there was a lot of intentionality in seeking out other Black women like themselves."

Dr. Leath's study found that these affinity groups not only offer a special kind of support, but they help Black women to navigate their own identity development.

Sharing a sense of sameness is about so much more than having similar music tastes—it's about getting affirmation about who we are.

But strange things happen when there are changes in our areas of sameness.

When we begin to lose this feeling, that's when conflict arises. It happens when someone:

- has a baby
- gets married
- leads a sober lifestyle after years of drinking together
- adopts a new faith
- gets sucked into the world of conspiracy theories (!!!)

Sharing worldviews, beliefs, and lifestyles helps us feel affirmed and understood, and while we'd like to think strong friendships can overcome anything, some changes feel too great to overcome.

But a desire for too much symmetry is also a problem. While a lack of sameness might challenge our sense of connection, craving *too much* similarity is also a threat to our sense of autonomy. When one friend expects the other to be just like her in every way, she'll get upset when her friend's choices don't mirror her own. So, she judges and criticizes, which leaves no room for her friends to be independent women with their own mind.

In any friendship, our degrees of sameness will fluctuate over time as we each grow and evolve. But it is up to us to determine the areas where we seek similarities while also holding space for each other's differences.

A lack of similarity separates; too much suffocates.

"Is she competing with me?"

Another way we experience symmetry is through equality. Women often endure unfair power dynamics in so many domains of their lives (in motherhood, marriage, and the workplace). This makes it especially important to have peers who will fight alongside us, shoulder to shoulder. We expect friends to fulfill that role.

This is why competition and envy feel like such terrible offenses in female friendship. If a friend competes with you, it reflects a desire to be better than you, disrupting the very egalitarianism that the friendship needs to thrive.

Sure, we expect that women will generally compete for resources—beating out other moms for a spot at the best school, being selected for the promotion over other women who applied—but there's an understanding that that kind of striving will take place outside the sacred safety of friendship.

Criticism and judgment also challenge our symmetry in this way, because having a friend constantly critique your choices sends a message that she sees her views as superior to yours. Over time, this positions her as the mentor/therapist/parent, and you as the mentee/client/child.

When we "other" our friends, it poses a threat to the sense of symmetry we need to feel seen, respected, and understood—prerequisites to connection.

"I feel like I'm the giver."

Reciprocity is the final component of the Symmetry Affinity and refers to equal prioritization and mutual contribution. In simple terms, we feel secure when we know that our friends put us first and that they're matching our efforts.

One of the top three issues I hear during private coaching sessions is, "I feel like I initiate more than my friends." When we suspect that we're giving more (of our time, energy, finances, emotional bandwidth), it makes us question the validity of the friendship. We grow fearful that we're being taken advantage of, worried that we're not cared for the way we thought we were.

There's nothing more upsetting in a friendship than harboring the suspicion that you're more invested than your friend is, and it tips the scales of reciprocity that feels so crucial to connection.

Without reciprocity, a woman may begin to feel like a pursuer. A nuisance. An unrequited lover.

It's so startling when tensions emerge in Symmetry because when we initially establish a connection, there's this unspoken contract of terms we've agreed to: "We relate in the following ways, and because of this, we are friends." When something shifts (either inside or outside the friendship), we have to renegotiate those terms to keep the friendship going.

Whenever different life seasons or beliefs threaten the ways in which you feel that you can relate to one another, it's important to identify other ways you two are similar. As long as you two believe you're the same in certain ways, it can keep you connected.

While some friendships won't go the distance, we can increase our chances of connection and understanding when we identify similarities, maintain equality, and exercise reciprocity.

Affinity 2: Secrecy

The Secrecy Affinity centers on **mutual sharing** and **exclusivity**. Together, they form a sort of "vault" where each friend contributes private things in an intimate and trustworthy space. In this space, they reveal themselves to one another, creating a sense of closeness and connection.

Limited access to the "vault" is the very thing that makes it feel so safe—we expect that what we share (vulnerabilities, fears, and experiences) will be protected, valued, and ultimately function to bring us closer.

Women's friendships tend to involve more self-disclosure than men's friendships, which accounts for the intimacy we often feel with one another. Over time, an attachment is formed, and because our friendships are mostly dyadic (between two people), that bond may feel even more intimate than it would be if it were divided among multiple people (group bonds).

Sharing something with a woman you just met can help you establish a friendship. Offering information about yourself, your family, your fears or flaws helps foster an affection and—because of something known as the "law of reciprocity"—she'll likely share something about herself in return.

In existing friendships, sharing can signal trust and create depth. We share by making verbal confessions and by inviting other women into our lives. We share our art with them, invite them into our home, and offer myriad other gestures that reveal more of who we are.

As our friends are entrusted with our secrets and experiences, it develops a loyalty within them. And this is how we form alliances.

"I feel that I don't know her anymore..."

Since women value equality and reciprocity, tensions may arise when one woman feels that she's sharing more than another. (*Why hasn't she shared much about her life when I've told her so much about mine?*) Since sharing is a display of trust, if she senses a "withholding" it can make her wonder whether there is a lack of trust in the friendship. And if a friend doesn't initiate sharing, she may risk being viewed as apathetic. (*Why doesn't she ever call/text me first?*)

If a woman discovers, for example, that a friend didn't confide in her about a personal hardship or success, she may be inclined to wonder whether her friend is drifting away, and whether that withholding was due to lack of care or trust.

Withholding can also call your closeness into question, and this suspicion isn't without merit. Oftentimes, an indicator that we are no longer interested in maintaining a friendship is to begin measuring what we share.

Openness is an invitation to the vault; withholding feels like exclusion.

But can there ever be *too much* sharing?

It's not uncommon to hear a woman lament falling into the role of "therapist" for her friend. Conflict arises when the frequency and intensity of sharing throws things off balance. There's resentment in being bridled with the weight of someone's disclosure if the recipient feels uncomfortable, unequipped, or uninterested, and this often results in her distancing herself from the source of her tension.

And remember, so much of this is relative. One person might be sharing to the degree that she is comfortable while her friend determines whether it's enough. The "sweet spot" is always when two friends are on the same page about how much they want to offer and how they prioritize each other. It will always look different from each woman's vantage point, according to her expectations, needs, and the season of life that she finds herself in. Open communication is how we recalibrate.

There's power in who you choose to share with; it marks the difference between friends and nonfriends. Having exclusivity in the "vault" is what makes the relationship special. Developing inside jokes and sharing unique experiences reassures us that our unique bond can't be duplicated somewhere else.

When we tell a friend about a hardship we're facing, we signal to her that she's special because she's been selected as a confidante. The assumption is that we are not having the same conversation with fifty other people, because if we were, the act of sharing becomes diluted, meaningless. Having top-tier access makes us feel important and highly prioritized. Exclusivity functions to form and maintain alliances.

"Why didn't she tell me first?"

But the Secrecy Affinity can feel violated when a friend passes our information to someone outside of the vault. Conflict can also arise when a friend shares big news (a pregnancy, promotion, health diagnosis) with someone else before telling us. Intellectually, we know we're not entitled to first dibs on every minor life development, but when we don't get it, we might find ourselves questioning our closeness.

We may also feel a sense of tension when a friend begins to make new friends. Sure, we know that we don't have ownership over the women we love, and that it's actually *healthy* for them to develop an expansive social network. But our desire to maintain the exclusivity that brings us so much intimacy may be threatened when another woman enters the picture.

And the jealousy we feel during those moments may not be a bad thing.

Dr. Jaimie Arona Krems is a social psychologist whose research focuses on female sociality. One of her more popular studies[20] shines a light on how friendship jealousy can actually be beneficial. She and her team found that feeling nervous that someone else will take your friend (it sounds juvenile but, alas, we've all been there!) simply shows us that the friendship is something we value. And those feelings of jealousy—while uncomfortable to experience—can inspire acts of preservation that motivate us to do what it takes to keep the friendship strong (or at least out of the grips of someone else's hands). So, although the inspiration to pour into our friendships may come from a fear of losing them to someone else, it can still be effective in getting us to do the work required to maintain the relationship.

Honoring the exclusivity aspect of the Secrecy Affinity helps create depth, trust, and intimacy over time.

Affinity 3: Support

This friendship affinity involves providing support through **emotional help** and **demonstrations of solidarity.**

Research[21] shows that emotional support is the number one trait women look for in a same-sex friendship. The essence of friendship, for most women, is to be connected with someone who can provide loving encouragement and compassion for her throughout life's highs and lows.

When I met my friend Stefania, we bonded over having toddlers and running a business. Our first offers of support to one another were mild enough: sharing links to parenting podcasts and exchanging business advice.

But we opened up to each other over the next year, and she gradually became one of the most beautiful people I know. Everything I learned about her endeared me to her even more, and I found myself wanting to give her anything I could—my time, my counsel, my energy. I was suddenly looking for opportunities to support her as a demonstration of my love, answering late-night calls without feeling inconvenienced and planning extensive self-care days at her mere mention of being overwhelmed by work.

Supporting her felt like a privilege, not a burden. And she returned my attentiveness and care, speaking life into me on days when I was discouraged.

We were attuned to each other's need for support, largely because we were able to read and respond to subtle cues and subtext. We spoke the same language.

But this can spell trouble for women who aren't especially fluent in the rules and language of emotional support.

Amanda Holmstrom is an associate professor in the Department of Communication at Michigan State University. Her research mainly focuses on communication and social support in relationships.

"It turns out that women evaluate women who provide low-quality support (saying things like 'Get over it' or 'It's not that big of a deal') more poorly. They don't like them as much, and don't see their comfort as effective. You kind of might expect your boyfriend or husband to not be able to support you in that way, but when you go to your girlfriends, you expect them to tend to your feelings and validate them."

Dr. Holmstrom also found that in communication areas like listening and conflict management, women didn't show a difference in what they expected from men or women. But when it came to comfort and emotional support, they had higher expectations for women than they had for men.

I wonder whether this issue is only compounded by our tendency to avoid explicitly telling friends what we want, since we believe they should just know. So, if things don't go well when we're in need of a friend's support, we are less likely to attribute it to our lack of communication, and more inclined to review it as a result of her inadequacies.

"By and large, people are not providing bad support on purpose. In fact, they often think they're doing a good job. So, when your girlfriend doesn't say or do what you'd hoped, sometimes we get in our head: 'She doesn't care!' But usually people don't know better. They don't know how to provide support."

We would eliminate so many misunderstandings and silent breaches if we acknowledged the idea of "support" as a subjective, elusive shapeshifter that presents itself differently to different women at different times.

What qualifies as support and to what extent? I've had countless women tell me they suspect their friends aren't genuine because they never comment on their social media stories or like their posts (no, this is not just younger women—it's middle-aged women, too). Or perhaps we expect support to look like initiating phone calls or having prompt responses to texts. Maybe we expect a friend to make a personal visit when we're sick, instead of sending soup over. Maybe we want her support to look like extended quiet during our vent session, even though she believes she's being helpful by offering solutions.

While you expected your friend to support you purchasing a mug from your new pottery business, she thought she was being helpful by sharing about your new venture on social media.

While you expected your friend to let you talk about your fears after a breakup, she decided to support you by encouraging you to dress up and go into town, to distract you from thinking about your loser ex.

And this is typically where I'm hit with the phrase: "But, Danielle, she should know. If she's really my friend, I shouldn't have to spell it out. It should be obvious."

I get that. But our friends aren't mind readers. Even when it comes to something that we feel should be obvious and intuitive like how to show up for us, we have to realize that we'll never achieve a level of closeness that transcends the need to communicate.

Linguist Deborah Tannen describes it best using what she calls the "Birthday Present Dilemma."

When your birthday is approaching, you hope that you get the gifts you want. You don't want to have to tell others what you want because them *knowing* what to get you is evidence of how well they know you. But if you don't tell them what to get you, you run the risk of not getting what you want.

Would our friends show up differently if they had access to all of the information? If we simply made it plain?

The idea that we shouldn't have to explain what we need to real friends is a relationship-killing myth. When we have high expectations that we're unwilling to communicate, there will forever be a gap between what we want and what we're getting.

Support looks different for everyone, but there seems to be an expectation that a woman will download and subscribe to her friend's interpretation in order to prove her allegiance. The question becomes how to balance a sense of agency with the responsibility to show up for a friend when it's inconvenient or contradictory to what you believe.

Finding Alignment and "Instinct Blindness"

Laureon Merrie is a doctoral candidate at the Oklahoma Center for Evolutionary Analysis, and much of her research centers around female conflict and competition.

"Women don't want to hear that women's friendships are fragile and that they're not forgiving of certain transgressions, and we may have the tendency to push back on it and say, 'Well, I'm not like that,' but I think most of us are more like that than we realize.

"It's what evolutionary psychologists refer to as *instinct blindness*. You don't know that it's happening because it's a part of your evolved instincts. You don't have to consciously think about it, but you're doing it anyway. It's sort of a program that's running in the back of your mind."

You may dismiss some female tendencies that have been outlined in these Friendship Affinities as not applicable to you, and that may be true. But as you move forward in platonic relationships with other women, pay close attention to your raw initial reaction to certain things she says and does and how you initially emotionally respond.

The first step toward finding alignment with a friend is to be able to identify (and then articulate) values you may not have considered before: how emotional support is offered, reciprocal self-disclosure, maintaining a "shared reality" on issues that matter most to you.

Remember, the longer two women have been friends and the closer they are, there's more room for variability in these affinities. When we're close, we expect our friend to challenge us, push back, and be honest even when it hurts. Healthy relationships thrive on that. But along the way, each friend gets to dictate the forms and degrees of support, secrecy, and symmetry she needs in her friendships.

For the gaps we find difficult to reconcile, we get to choose whether to accept the friendship as it is or to work through ways to form better alignment.

We always have the right to choose whether we want to make the accommodations and compromises necessary to make a friendship work.

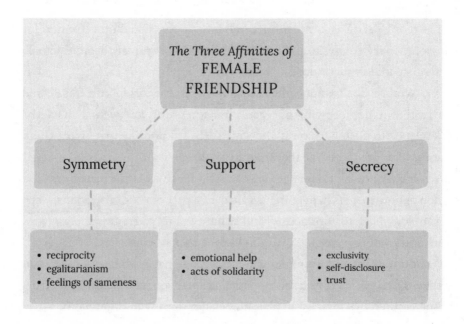

Chapter 2 Questions

1. Think of a conflict you recently had with a friend. Which one of the Three Affinities was at the heart of your issue?
2. Have you ever had a friend become dissatisfied with your level of support, despite your best efforts to show up for her?
3. In a friendship, what do you do when you notice a gap between what you want and what you're getting? How do you manage and communicate those expectations?

Chapter 3 Preview Question

When you are disappointed with a friend, how do you typically address the issue?

Chapter 3

Healthy Conflict and Platonic Intimacy

What Doesn't Kill You Makes You Closer

I think about her sometimes.

Roshana and I met while teaching together at one of the county's largest high schools. I broke the ice by making an inappropriate joke during lunch in the teacher's lounge, and when she laughed, I knew I wanted to be her friend.

That exchange began a two-year whirlwind of erratic texts, late-night clubbing, and shared last-minute lesson plans. We were baptized together and supported each other through messy cycles of making up and breaking up with guys who honestly weren't even worth our time.

We vented about failures in the education system while tossing around the idea of writing a book about our online dating experiences. The friendship had range.

But things exploded one night over a giant misunderstanding.

One night, I found myself stressed from working sixty hours during "testing week" at school, and was behind on grading papers. I thought about how relaxing it would be to smoke a joint (even though I'd only smoked twice before in my life: once to prove to my college boyfriend that I wasn't a square, and again at an Outkast concert). I felt conflicted because I didn't grow up with that kind of thing being okay, and I generally believe in living a sober lifestyle. But I was so tense and overwhelmed that I threw that out the window and soon began scrolling through my contacts to see whether I knew anyone who could secretly hook me up.

That's when I saw Michael's number.

Roshana had a best friend named Tiana, and Michael was her on-again, off-again boyfriend. I'd only ever spent time with him when we would hang out in large groups. I didn't know much about him except that he was funny, and that he made occasional references to smoking.

This is when I had the bright idea to text him to see whether he could swing by to drop off some weed. I felt a pit in my stomach because it felt like I was breaking a major code to invite Tiana's sometimes-boyfriend to my house. Alone. At night.

But in the moment, I'd convinced myself it wasn't a big deal because it was strictly business.

Michael came over and we smoked.

I immediately felt ashamed. If I was doing something I didn't want my friends to find out about, something was wrong. So, I sent him on his way and tried to block it out of my mind.

Little did I know that Michael and Tiana shared an Uber account. This meant that if he went anywhere, she knew about it.

The next morning, I got a phone call from Roshana. Tiana was screaming in the background, saying something about my trying to steal her boyfriend and calling me a few other choice words. Roshana demanded to know what had happened, growing increasingly suspicious of my story.

I tried to explain to them that I only invited Michael over for weed, but they didn't believe me. Initially, I was embarrassed and apologetic, but then I became indignant. Why didn't Roshana believe me? She knew me better than most people, so the fact that the character I'd demonstrated to her over the past two years suddenly meant nothing was hurtful. I could accept her telling me that it was a bad move, sure. But to accuse me of actually being with somebody else's man? If she thought I'd do something so low, I wondered whether she even really knew me at all.

And why wasn't she advocating for me to Tiana? Maybe she couldn't defend what I did, but she could at least speak up and help me convince her that nothing went down. The fact that Roshana didn't do that made me feel that she chose her over me, and it hurt.

There were tears, accusations, and apologies...and that launched us into months of not speaking to each other. It was painful to lose a good friend, but it hurt even more to know that it was because of a decision that I made.

At one point, we arranged to meet up for lunch, but the conversation was awkward. As much as I wanted us to jump back to the way we were before, I knew that the friendship as we knew it was over.

This happened more than seven years ago, and even though we live in the same city, I haven't seen her since.

What hurts most is the regret. Before Roshana, my friendships either ended because I released them or because there was a mutual, drama-free fade-out. This felt like the first time a friendship ended because of *my* mistakes.

Looking back, I see Roshana as my platonic "one that got away." I toss her onto the pile of "former friendships" I've collected throughout my lifetime, along with:

- the roommate turned bestie that I eventually outgrew
- the college friend who phased me out when she got a boyfriend
- the coworker bestie who disappeared from my life when I started working somewhere else
- the mom friend I grew close to but eventually lost trust in
- the friend I had to release because she didn't reach out enough
- the church friend who cut *me* I off because *I* didn't reach out enough

...and a slew of other friendships that dissolved because of time, distance, misunderstandings, and unspoken resentments. While I have a few friends I've known for more than a decade, there are some relationships that simply didn't survive along the way.

But how do we measure the success of a friendship? Is it one that never ends or one that served its purpose? And how do we fight for friendships that matter to us when tensions arise and threaten to tear us apart?

The Fragility of Women's Friendships

Research[22] finds that young women have more "prior friendships" than males, and a lower threshold for dealing with perceived violations. We're also more likely to be able to list something a current friend has already done "wrong," and we're less likely than men to reconcile after a falling-out.[23]

In a nutshell, female friendships are fragile.

Some of us are enjoying friendships that have lasted for decades, but there are still those friendships that seemed to have dissolved because somebody made a misstep (likely one she wasn't even aware of), and before we know it, the relationship's over.

But the research reveals a few reasons that women's friendships might be sensitive to conflict:

First, conflict is most likely to happen with people we're close to, and since women form intimate friendships, they experience more breakups. It seems counterintuitive at first—that more depth leads to more endings—but we simply aren't falling out with people we're not deeply invested in to begin with.

Another reason our friendships can be fragile (especially compared to men's friendships!) is because we have high expectations. A review of thirty-six studies[24] found that women wanted more from their close relationships than men did (especially when it comes to reciprocity and self-disclosure), which means we are setting—and expected to meet—high standards.

This means that we also register more relational violations, identifying more "wrongs" in our friendships. In one study, researchers observed college dorms to monitor the number of roommate reassignment requests. Most of them came from the women.

Dr. Joyce Benenson[25] led this research, and was surprised by what she found:

"The girls were complaining that their roommates weren't hygienic, they turned on the fan without asking permission, they talked too loudly on the phone... The men were just not complaining. And then I objectively looked at that and I couldn't believe it."

She theorizes that because women are tasked with so much—whether in the workplace or in the home (for many women, in both spheres)—investing in a non-kin female relationship is an "opportunity cost." So, when we do get involved, it means a lot and we integrate our lives. But since society burdens us with so many responsibilities, there's less tolerance for enduring stress betrayal from friends.

"Females are very selective and very careful about their relationships. And for good reason: we're so responsible, so conscientious... we're trying to do the best we can for ourselves, for our families," Benenson writes. Still, one of the greatest barriers to creating more resilient friendships is our relationship with conflict itself.

As a millennial raised on shows like *Bad Girls Club* and 297 seasons of *Real Housewives*, I used to associate conflict in female friendship with yelling, gossiping, and table-flipping. And while that's definitely one version of conflict, it's not the *healthy* kind.

Because *healthy* conflict with friends is inevitable.

When you enter a friendship, you're bringing your needs, goals, boundaries, and desires to the table—and so is she! At some point, there will be a clash because you'll have competing interests, and you'll need to get to the business of working it out.

That "clash" has a really important function: it's an opportunity to meet a need, solve a problem, and deepen our friendships. The more we get to know each other, the more opportunity there is for conflict.

When you meet a new friend, everything is great. You quickly discover all that you have in common and, while you don't know each other well, the chemistry is all-consuming. But the closer you get, the better you can see her faults and uncover differences—conflict becomes inevitable.

The problem is that so many of us see the idea of conflict itself as contradictory to friendship. But research[26] shows that it's not conflict itself that ends relationships—it's the *outcome* from the conflict.

When you get it right, healthy conflict will lead to decreased anxiety, increased understanding, and increased closeness. But negative outcomes may include anger and anxiety, decreased satisfaction, and withdrawal.

Healthy Conflict vs. Unhealthy Conflict

We enter romantic relationships *knowing* that there will be trials along the way; we don't have the same anticipation in our friendships.

But friendship is a relationship, and any relationship worth having requires work.

So, how do we make sure we're doing conflict right?

First, it's important to be able to differentiate healthy conflict from unhealthy conflict.

Unhealthy conflict works *against* connection and often puts individual ego before the needs of the relationship. Healthy conflict, by contrast, works to find solutions. While it might be uncomfortable in the short term, it has productive long-term outcomes.

UNHEALTHY CONFLICT CAN LOOK LIKE:	
• giving the silent treatment • talking to everyone else about your issue instead of speaking directly to your friend about it • denying your feelings of discomfort to "keep the peace"	• immediately withdrawing (physically or emotionally) in an effort to protect yourself • manipulation through blaming, guilting, gaslighting, or shaming • defending and justifying instead of listening
HEALTHY CONFLICT:	
• may hurt, but is never intentionally hurtful • knows how to take ownership and apologize • takes turns, allowing each person to have a say	• wants to collaboratively attack the issue, not the person • makes attempts to repair • doesn't put individual goals first • honors the other person's boundaries

Healthy conflict may look like two friends disagreeing on an issue but trying to find a way to relate to each other in spite of those divergent perspectives. With healthy conflict in your friendship, it's not you against your friend; it's you and your friend against the problem.

So many of us are ill equipped to navigate these moments. And it's no surprise why.

Learning to Fight

For many of us, it began in childhood. Think about the playground spats you brought to teachers or parents only to be met with generic advice like "Be nice." Then, we went to middle school, and our attempts to seek mediation were dismissed with simple justifications like "She's just jealous. Stop hanging out with her." As a teenager, you may have swallowed your feelings for the sake of belonging, or—depending on your culture or family norms—you may have been encouraged to fight her or cuss her out.

So many of us have a dysfunctional approach to conflict with friends because we were coached by authority figures to either ignore the issue or attack to maintain dominance. In that kind of climate, the idea of gently but directly making our needs known, working together to find a solution, and vulnerably admitting our fears and failings are foreign concepts.

In the moment, it seems easier to either end the friendship or stay and pretend there aren't any issues. We don't want to risk being seen as difficult, sensitive, or dramatic. We don't want to risk being misunderstood or abandoned. (We'll examine the reasons for and consequences of conflict avoidance in Chapter 4.)

It doesn't help that some of us see conflict with friends as a sign of incompatibility. So, when a friend disappoints us and things get tense, we begin to question her character altogether. While this may be true in some circumstances, conflict itself is not a revelation of some fundamental incongruence, or evidence that we weren't meant to be friends.

Some conflicts will expose differences too great to overcome, but others get us one step closer toward experiencing platonic intimacy.

Conflict as Intimacy

The words *chemistry, closeness,* and *intimacy* are sometimes used interchangeably. But they're not the same.

Chemistry is when you experience a natural rhythm with someone. This is something you can have within two seconds of meeting, and it doesn't require you to have any real knowledge of the person's character.

Closeness is what happens once you start to get knowledge of someone. You learn about them and feel the Symmetry Affinity begin to take root through what you've discovered, and that knowledge makes you feel connected.

This is why we sometimes don't feel close to our friends when we're arguing—it challenges the rhythm of chemistry and disorients us from what we thought we knew about the person. But once we talk things through, we can feel realigned and there's room for the closeness to return.

But platonic intimacy is on a whole new level.

Harriet Lerner, a psychologist and relationship expert breaks it all down in her book *The Dance of Intimacy*:[27]

> It is when we stay in a relationship over time…that our capacity for intimacy is put to the test. It's only in long-term relationships that we're called upon to navigate that delicate balance between separateness and togetherness, and that we confront the challenge of sustaining both.

Platonic intimacy means you have the freedom to show up as your authentic self while allowing your friend to do the same. This means you can share your vulnerabilities and your weaknesses, without a fear of rejection; and when your friend opens up to you, you resist the urge to try to change her.

I can't help to think about my friend Quanna when I talk about platonic intimacy. She is the ultimate example of what it means to be all in in friendship. Quanna is one of the most loyal people I know, and when anything good happens in my life, she's moved to actual tears, telling me I make her proud. A large part of the reason I feel smart and capable is that she sees this in me. And I want to be the woman she believes me to be.

But she has also witnessed my ugliness. Quanna has listened without judgment as I've flipped into a rage, and she's had front-row seats to twenty years' worth of questionable decisions. In those moments, she never pulls away. She never shames me. She calls me to a high standard, reminding me of the best parts of myself, and demands that I show up in my greatness.

While I was writing this book, we recently experienced a conflict on a subject we view very differently. She shared her opinion on the matter with great respect and care, and I'm not going to lie—it was uncomfortable for us both. We were on the phone, and I began pacing back and forth while we were talking, and it literally became difficult to breathe.

And she knows me well:

"Why are you breathing like that?"
"Um, because this whole thing is really intense but I'm also really glad you're finally telling me how you feel."

The call ended with our saying, "I love you," and I hung up wondering whether we would be okay.

The following week, we went to the Improv together—a date we'd committed to before our disagreement. During the show, we laughed and had a good time, but as we walked to our cars afterward, I still felt a little tense inside.

"Hey, I know our conversation last week was kinda crazy. I just wanna make sure we're good."
"Girl, yes. We're good."

Things got pretty meta as we proceeded to have a conversation *about* the conversation, to make sure there was clarity and understanding between us. And you know what? After twenty years of friendship, it unlocked another layer of closeness. The conflict produced positive outcomes that included a certain intimacy, and showed us there is freedom and safety to bring our full selves to the table without fear of abandonment, misunder-standing, or retaliation. It increased our respect for each other and con-firmed that it's one of the most valued relationships in my life.

My friendship with Quanna feels like home. It is worth fighting for.

Real friendship doesn't feel like a performance. There's safety to bring all of who you are.

With every healthy conflict we successfully resolve, we feel more heard and learn more about the other person. We get closer to experiencing pla-tonic intimacy.

And while we won't be able to elevate every friendship to this level, it helps to understand what it looks like and develop the skill of navigating difficult times to position us to enjoy greater depth with the women we love.

Healthy conflict is a prerequisite to platonic intimacy.

Can We Go the Distance?

How do you know whether a specific issue is worth raising?

First, we have to remember that not every friendship has a capacity for platonic intimacy. If you're dealing with a friend who is defensive, pes-simistic, abusive, or who carries any ill-intent toward you, it's going to be difficult to enjoy this kind of relationship with them. This is also true of people-pleasers who are scared to show up as themselves, which will affect the degree to which they will ever be known within that friendship.

Navigating healthy conflict brings us platonic intimacy, but it also requires each of us to deal with our own "stuff."

While it's important to have general conflict resolution skills, we're constantly evaluating what's worth addressing, and with whom. The next time you're trying to determine whether to lean in to safe and healthy con-flict, ask yourself the following questions:

What is the weight of the offense? Let's keep it real: How serious is the issue? Reflect on whether you're verbalizing every discomfort or the matter at hand needs to be addressed. Know the difference between a friend with obnoxious habits and behaviors that have the potential to cause real hurt to you or the relationship overall.

What's the frequency? How often is the issue occurring, and what effect does the frequency have on the relationship? If a friend who's usually on time is late to your big event (and apologizes!), do you have a formal sit-down about the ways you feel disrespected? Is a friend's ongoing mistreatment something you dismiss and accept as her "just being herself"? Evaluate one-time behavior and reoccurring actions that cause distress and use discernment to determine how you'd like to approach the situation and whether it requires anything on your end (e.g., firmer boundaries).

What is her reception to feedback? Can your friendship withstand addressing the conflict (and if not, does that say something)? Is your friend especially defensive? Is there evidence in your friendship history that feedback is welcome and productive, or is there little room to confidently and lovingly express a need? Over time, this may signal the health of the friendship overall.

How deep is our mutual interest and commitment? How important is this relationship to you? Do you want it to continue long term? Is your friend as invested as you are in the growth of the relationship? While you should advocate for your needs in your relationships, you may decide your connection is best as a light and loose acquaintanceship and not worth having heavier conversations.

The goal is to make sure we are equipped (both tangibly and emotionally) to work through issues with women whose friendship we value. And that starts with being able to differentiate between conflicts that will enhance the relationship, and those that genuinely aren't worth the battle.

The Four Barriers to Reconciliation Among Women

Now that we understand healthy conflict as a pathway to platonic intimacy, we have to identify behaviors that get in the way.

The Four Barriers to Reconciliation are tendencies women have that work against their being able to reconcile with a friend. The four barriers are **expectations, rumination, attribution, and lack of mediation**.

Let's look at how each of these affects friends' ability to return to each other after conflict.

Expectations

Much of conflict is a result of unmet expectations, which leads to disappointment.

The issue doesn't lie in *having* expectations, as that is how we set direction in our relationships and get our needs met. But it's what we do with our expectations that might be setting us up for unintended conflict.

A study by Anna Machin[28] found that women tend to have higher expectations than men when it comes to their close relationships, specifically in the areas of reciprocity and intimacy. But why do these expectations so often go unmet?

I think there are two beliefs that contribute to our disappointment.

First, we tend to say that we shouldn't have to tell our friends what we need because "they should know." This leads to disappointment and confusion as our friends are unfairly expected to be mind readers, and we are left continually dissatisfied.

Because of the Symmetry Affinity, we also tend to expect our friends to show up in the way that we show up. When they don't, we're surprised that their choices don't mirror our own. We have to hold space for our friends to operate differently than we do and bridge any gaps with open communication. This positions us to have more of the love and understanding that we're looking for.

Let's say your friend does or says something that turns you off. You find yourself thinking, *How could she say that/forget about that/think that? I would never do that. And I shouldn't have to say anything—she should know.* And then you begin to physically and emotionally distance yourself.

But if your friend had access to all the information that you're holding, would she have chosen differently?

If we don't take time to check in with ourselves and our relationships, we'll be surprised by the fissures that appear as a result of unmet expectations. Paying attention to them can help minimize the disappointment and the emotional distance that tend to follow.

Rumination

Rumination, in its simplest form, is to think about something deeply. But at its worst, it can become obsessive, repeatedly replaying, analyzing, and reflecting on a real or imagined event.

Deep thinking is helpful when we're carefully considering the right words to support a friend in distress. It's a critical aspect of our problem-solving superpowers as we carefully weigh which plan of action will cause as little harm as possible.

But intense rumination can also be counterproductive to working through an issue with a friend. Research suggests that women take a longer time to reconcile in their friendships than men do. Some of the delay might be due to women's tendency to ruminate[29] more than men do.

Attribution

I'm going to resist the temptation to write this section in all-caps, but I need you to know that I really want to because it's just that important:

Fundamental attribution theory is the tendency to see a person's actions as a reflection of their character, while attributing our *own* misdeeds or wrongdoings to external circumstances.

And I believe that this accounts for a major chunk of our issues.

Here's how it works:

Let's say your friend didn't return your call last week after promising that she would. You begin to ruminate and decide that she's being thoughtless and inconsiderate. *She never thinks of other people. She can be so self-absorbed.*

Yet when *you* fail to call or text a friend back, it's because something came up and you got distracted.

Another example: When your friend goes back to the boyfriend she swore off, you think, *Why is she being so weak? I hate that she puts her relationship over us. Why is her self-esteem so low that she can't be strong enough to leave him?* But when you start talking to *your* ex again, it's because you don't want to be rude and completely cut him off. Besides, he really needed help with this one thing, so it's not a big deal.

And yet another example: When your friend is thirty minutes late to brunch, you begin thinking about how rude it is for her to let you wait that long. *She's taking advantage of how nice I am.* But when *you're* late, it was because of... traffic.

We often attribute our friend's "wrongdoings" to a character deficiency while simultaneously justifying the times when we drop the ball. Since we already perceive more violations in our friendships than men do, the issue is only compounded by a tendency to associate those violations with failings in her character.

And since we value sameness and symmetry in our female friendships, we leave convinced that we aren't compatible, citing "irreconcilable differences" when the friendship ends.

Do you see how that can magnify a small, circumstantial (fixable) thing into a major source of emotional division?

And I wonder whether some of us are more prone to leaning into fundamental attribution theory because we are so good at reading subtext (which means we may find ourselves searching for the bigger meaning in a word or action). We also have strong intuition, so we think our observations and speculations about our friend's motive and character are spot on.

The key here is to explore whether it's helpful to extend the benefit of the doubt whenever a friend doesn't come through or to jump straight to assumptions and character demerits. This may allow us to move forward without the same sense of disconnection.

Lack of Mediation

The way that we do—or don't—seek mediation during conflict can greatly impact our chances at emotionally reconnecting with a friend we feel distanced from. Consider your tendency to seek the guidance and support of a third party during conflict, and ask yourself:

Am I looking for support and validation? Or do I want someone to hype me up when I list reasons for why my friend's being selfish right now? Many of us simply want to know that we're not "crazy," eager to test our experience against someone else's interpretation of events to see whether we have an accurate handle on what's going on.

We might also be trying to work out how we feel, brainstorming different scripts and ideas for how to return to our friend and address the issue. But we want to do it somewhere we feel safe enough to express how we really feel without judgment with a person we trust to help us through it. Someone we know will call us out when we're wrong or encourage us to advocate for ourselves. This can be helpful in gaining perspective.

But there are some situations where seeking third parties is unhelpful.

If we're going to outside groups to triangulate the experience (involving other people to create drama) or gossip about the friend we're falling out with, we're not seeking genuine mediation. When we engage in these kinds of behaviors, the objective is not to reconcile with our friend.

And some of us don't even have a third-party group to turn to, to help us mediate an issue with a friend.

A friendship dissolution study by Robin Dunbar[30] found that women tend to splinter off from larger networks and form one-on-one connections. But without the support, perspective, and objectivity that third parties offer, a relationship between two best friends is vulnerable during times of misunderstanding, and susceptible to erosion.

Whether we are a part of a friend trio or we simply have a strong network of supportive silo-friendships, talking through an issue with wise and well-intentioned others can be helpful in our efforts toward reconciliation.

How to Have the Hard Conversation

Once you've decided that you want to address an issue with a friend, the challenge becomes figuring out exactly how you want to approach her.

Initiating a hard conversation with a friend can feel so risky because we fear her reaction (*What if she pulls away? misunderstands me? gets upset?*) and the outcome (*What if we never recover? Is this the beginning of the end?*).

But there are ways to work through it while causing as little harm as possible—and possibly becoming closer than before.

Step 1. Regulate Your Emotions

Being able to emotionally cope with stress has a direct impact on the quality of your relationships. In our female friendships, there are countless moments when something is said or done and it stirs feelings that dictate our behavior.

How do you respond in moments of irritation and offense? What do you do when you're hurt?

Regulating your emotions involves reframing how you see the issue in front of you, and controlling what you do in response. Try your best to reappraise the situation when necessary, and accept things as they are. Then, get curious about what would be the most productive response.

When we struggle to regulate our emotions, we'll respond to perceived triggers in destructive ways, such as self-blaming, withdrawing, and catastrophizing.[31] This makes things worse because it takes us longer to reconcile, causes us to overreact, and leads us to become depressed and anxious.

The research also finds people who aren't able to regulate their emotions tend to receive others' feedback as hostile, "punish" people, cut people off, and exaggerate the negative aspects of manageable disagreements.

If you don't get your emotions in check, it will not only impact your capacity to even have a healthy conversation, but could seriously impact the trajectory of the friendship overall.

Step 2: Consider the Mind-Body Connection

In his book *More Than Words*,[32] John Howard outlines the problems with prioritizing communication over connection: before our brain can receive messages, our nervous system needs to be at rest.

Howard explains that before we can receive what a friend or loved one is saying to us, we first want to know: *Do you love me? Do you care? Do I matter to you?* It's within the context of these reassurances that we're better able to engage and connect.

We learn best when we feel safe.

If appropriate, try waiting until you and your friend are doing something fun, or when you're coming down from the high of a shared belly laugh. You might pause and slowly introduce the subject, waiting until you all are in a good place to embed your message in a pocket of connection.

Think about ways you can make sure your friend feels safe before you address your "hard thing." Consider your body language, the safety of your environment, and your tone. Be intentional about ways you can help her to know—verbally or otherwise—that she is safe and she matters to you before putting the issue on the table.

Step 3: Lean in to Vulnerability

Here's one exercise you can use to make sure you lead with vulnerability:

Think about the reason you're reluctant to have the conversation. (*You're nervous that she's going to blow up at you. You don't want her to go back and tell the rest of the friend group. You don't want to look like the bad guy. You don't want it to be awkward.*) Then, use that reason as one of your opening lines.

Together, it looks like:

"*Hey, I was reluctant to bring this up because the **last thing I want is for anything to be awkward between us**, but I thought it was worth mentioning anyway because I love it when you and I are on the same page, and I think that talking through this will help us understand each other better.*"

Admitting that you're nervous about having the conversation can bring her defenses down and position you as thoughtful and careful in your approach. It might also make her mindful of doing the behavior you said you were apprehensive about (having her pull away or lash out).

When you show a willingness to let down your guard, it's a demonstration of your willingness to release control, and now your friend can feel secure in knowing that the following conversation is not one of a power dynamic, but that you're coming to her as a peer who's invested in the friendship.

Step 4. Let Curiosity Drive the Conversation

Sometimes, before we approach a friend with a tough issue, we've prepared a list of all the points we want to make, but this can mean that we've made assumptions that leave no room for her perspective.

Intellectual humility is a phrase that refers to the degree to which someone accepts that they could be wrong.[33] People with intellectual humility make more thoughtful decisions, have stronger connections with others, and are happier overall compared to those without this mind-set.

Think about how open you are to learning about your friend's perspective to better inform your feelings and behavior.

Research[34] shows that one of the most powerful predictors of how a disagreement will turn out is how the parties perceive each other's receptiveness. If your friend is not convinced that you're actually open to hearing what she has to say, you might be setting yourself up for an unproductive conversation.

Some phrases that can demonstrate your receptiveness:

"I see where you're coming from..."
"It's clear that we both care about..."
"I appreciate the way you..."
"I never considered that..."

When we believe that the person we're in conflict with is open to our perspective and has a desire to learn, we're more willing to be receptive to them.

Step 5. Focus on the Impact, Not the Behavior

If you go to your friend armed with a list of all the things she's done wrong, she's going to try to defend herself. Before you know it, you all are involved in a messy back-and-forth that becomes more of a debate than a conversation.

To minimize the spirit of defensiveness, try to focus on the impact of her behavior instead of the behavior itself.

So, instead of saying, "You're always late," you might try, "When we don't get started on time, it throws off the timeline for the rest of the night and it's really hard to get back on track."

If your complaint is that she's always making playful "digs" about how reckless you were back in your college days in front of other people, you might try, "When everyone gets together to hang out and there are jokes about my messy college days, I get embarrassed because I'd really rather not relive them. I know y'all are just playing around, but it makes me cringe because it doesn't really have much to do with who I am today."

A friend can defend her actions (*"What? I was just kidding. I didn't mean it like that."*), but it's difficult for her to contest your experience of her actions. Whether she agrees with your evaluation of her behavior, she can't deny the impact, and hopefully she's willing to make changes so that you feel safe, loved, and valued.

Step 6. Offer "Listener Checkpoints"

Since a conversation is made up of a series of verbal exchanges, it helps to make sure you interpret your friend's words in the same way that she intended them. Otherwise, you're responding to messages she's not even giving you! To prevent misunderstanding and minimize frustration, have checkpoints where you rephrase her point back to her, just to make sure you're getting it right. Yes, it requires a certain level of humility to acknowledge you don't know everything, and it shows her that you care enough to get it right.

Example A

You tell your friend that her temper is out of control and it makes it hard for you to talk to her.

She: "Well, I only yelled because you weren't listening to me and it really pissed me off. It annoys me so bad when you act like you know everything."

You: "So, you're saying that you feel like I'm not really hearing you, and that's what makes you react so strongly." [Rephrasing her statement without sarcasm or judgmental language.]

She: [Sighs, drops shoulders in relief that you finally understand her side] "Yes. I know I shouldn't pop off like that, but I can't deal with you overtalking me."

What you want to say next: "Yep, well throwing tantrums as a thirty-year-old woman is pretty crazy, and maybe that's why all your friends have left you and your blood pressure is through the roof."

What you actually say next: "I know how it feels to not be heard and it's superfrustrating, I agree. It's also hard for me to stay in a situation where someone is yelling at me like I'm a child. So, I'm trying to figure out how we can hear each other better without things getting so intense, because I know that next time that happens, I'm going to have to walk away."

Example B

You've told your friend that you don't appreciate the way she cancels plans with you every time her boyfriend asks her to spend time together.

She: "He has a crazy schedule, so I have to take whatever time I can get. It's not personal."

You: "So, you feel like you're not able to commit to decisions because your availability is dependent on his availability." [Rephrasing her point.]

She: "Yes, exactly."

What you want to say next: "Oh, I'm sorry, I didn't realize that you like being at his beck and call and that you want to put some random man ahead of your long-term friendships. Guess we lost another woman to the patriarchy!"

What you actually say next: "I hear you, and that must put you in a tough position. I know you care about us both, but when you don't follow through with our plans, it feels like you don't respect my time, and the story I start to tell myself is that you don't prioritize our friendship in the same way you do that relationship. Can we figure out a way that you can spend time with him but also avoid canceling plans with me?"

Summarizing her point doesn't mean you're giving in to her side. It just confirms your understanding and shows you care, and—according to the research—makes her more receptive to hearing *you.*

Be intentional about moving the conversation toward a place where each person feels understood and is reassured that the friendship matters.

Then, you can get to the work of collaboratively generating a plan for how to overcome the issue—together.

Step 7. End by Collaboratively Working Toward a Solution to Move Forward

It's important to remember that addressing something with a friend shouldn't be done with the goal of changing the other person. It's about solving a problem. If you want the conversation to work for you, you have to get to a point where you focus on how things can be different moving forward, minimizing the chances that this uncomfortable issue doesn't recur.

Let's say your friend is consistently late and you bring it up using this four-part method:

"I wasn't going to mention this because the last thing I want is for you to misunderstand where I'm coming from, but I thought it could actually be helpful to understanding the full picture. Sometimes, when we don't meet up at the time we scheduled, I get anxious because I never know when you're going to arrive, and then it throws off my plans for the rest of the night. So, I'm curious about what's going on on your end. Do the times we plan not really work for you? Or are we meeting up at places that are too far away from your house?"

The final task is to come up with something that works for everyone in the future. Perhaps, as with this situation, you agree to change where you meet up or she can agree to notify you, as soon as she senses her timeline is off, that's she's going to be late. Or maybe you both can start meeting up at a time that's more conducive for both your schedules.

This helps to establish a harmonious goal for your conversation, and works to advance the relationship by communicating needs and realigning expectations.

How to Say Hard Things: Digital Edition

These days, so much of our conversation takes place in a digital sphere, and while that's helpful in coordinating plans or maintaining long-distance relationships, it can be an unsuspecting culprit in the dissolution of friendships everywhere.

Some of us head straight to texts or direct messages when we want to communicate with a friend, giving little thought to the many factors that must be carefully considered beforehand.

You might be thinking, *But, Danielle, we're talking about texting my friend, not crafting an email to my boss.* I'm telling you: that reflexive impulse to grab the phone to send a message to a friend during a moment of conflict or confusion can be the match that sets everything on fire.

Think I'm being dramatic?

I can't tell you how many sessions I've had where a client is outlining the series of digital exchanges that lead to a falling-out.

Why does this happen? Is it just a matter of women who are too sensitive? Is this about our tendency to overanalyze? Are they being "petty," choosing to make something out of nothing?

The real issue at the heart of these scenarios is a lack of awareness over "digital body language." The phrase "digital body language" was coined by Erica Dhawan, an executive leader and author who teaches twenty-first-century collaboration skills to leaders across the world. The same way we communicate our feelings and intentions in person through physical body language (head nodding to show agreement; sighing to show boredom; eye rolls to express contempt), is how we communicate our messages in a digital sphere through other means. Here are a few aspects of digital body language that work together to impact our intended audience:

Brevity—If you send an essay-style text response, your friend may interpret that as being thoughtful or as dramatic and intense. Send her a two-word response (because you're in the middle of a meeting), and you may risk the assumption that you're being curt because you're upset.

Use of emojis and punctuation—Using emojis can be interpreted as playful or trivializing. They can function as softeners for otherwise intense messages and they can infuse personality into text that is dry.

Mode—We have so many avenues to communicate with our friends— social media direct messages, texts, emails. Does it matter which one we choose? Some could say that the medium you choose can say something about the seriousness, formality, and urgency of your message. And if you switch your mode of communication midconversation, this can have implications as well.

Response time—The amount of time that passes from when you send a message to when a friend responds may not matter in some circumstances. But delays can be read as avoidance, power plays, and lack of care. And quick responses can be seen as attentive, anxious, or controlling. Having different expectations about what qualifies as a reasonable response time can also be grounds for conflict, as a message that comes too late can be seen as rude, and demands for constant, immediate contact could be seen as having little regard for the other person's time.

I hate to say it, but it doesn't matter if, when your friend gets offended, you "didn't mean it like that." Intention is important, but it will always come second to the impact. And the *way* you communicate it has a lot of influence over how your message is received. So, we have the responsibility of communicating with clarity and consideration for the other person's experience of our words.

When trying to determine whether to communicate your message digitally or not, think about how your method of communication either advances or takes away from your message. Make sure there is as little room as possible for misinterpretation.

Now, if there's one thing I've learned from posting tips and strategies on social media, it's that there's inevitably going to be a comment from someone pointing out the ways in which certain aspects of this strategy won't work for them.

The key is to identify elements of this approach that might work for you and your friendships, and then get creative in adapting the rest to fit your lifestyle, personality, and friendship history.

When You're in the Hot Seat

There will be times that you're on the receiving end of what feels like a "callout." How you respond can make the difference between strengthening your friendship or creating tension and division.

So, when a woman you love comes to you and points out an issue she has with your words, actions, or attitude, here's how to handle it.

While it might feel cringe-worthy to get feedback about the impact of your behavior, remember that it's necessary to know how your actions affect others and to get data on how to better love your friends.

Here are a few tips to receive your friend when she raises an issue with you.

First, please know that you don't have to respond right away. Give yourself a break. Some of our defensiveness comes from an internal pressure to respond immediately. It's okay to say, "Wow, I had no idea you felt that way. I think I'm going to need a minute to process that." Advocate for time to think through how you feel and how you want to approach your friend. Hopefully, she's willing to grant you that.

Then, you want to look at her feedback as data. It's very hard when emotions are involved, but if we train ourselves to depersonalize it by downloading the information as data that we can use on our ongoing journey toward continued self-improvement, it might be more helpful.

Once you hear your friend out, you might find that you don't agree with her. You might genuinely see things differently than she does and disagree with her assessment. It's okay to say, "I hear you and I definitely don't want to do anything that makes you feel that way. But I'm struggling to see myself in the picture you just painted of me. But I promise you I'm going to stay mindful of that and make sure I never intentionally put you in that position."

As long as you don't approach this with a combative tone, you have the right to disagree with her opinion—and to continue to like her anyway.

You should also measure the feedback you're getting against patterns of other people's observations. Have you heard this message before? If your siblings, partner, and coworkers are all saying the same thing to you, it might be worth listening to.

And finally, examine your friend's intentions. If she typically has your best interest at heart and loves to see you win, then assume she has positive intentions. Weigh this moment against the evidence she has shown you over the course of your friendship and allow yourself to soften knowing you're in the company of someone who cares about you.

Then, try to see the feedback as an *extension* of her love for you, instead of as a *contradiction* of that love.

Chapter 3 Questions

1. What models do you have of healthy conflict, if any?
2. Think about a time you struggled to regulate your emotions during a conflict. What happened, and what would you have done differently?
3. Review the Four Barriers to Reconciliation (expectations, rumination, attribution, and lack of mediation). Which barrier is the most challenging for you to overcome during times of conflict?

Chapter 4 Preview Question

Share a time when you completely avoided a conflict with a friend. What was the reason you decided not to address it?

Chapter 4

Stress, Loneliness, and Resentment

The Consequences of Conflict Avoidance

I was huddled under a restaurant awning, trying my best not to get drenched by the unpredictable Florida rain, when it hit me: *She's not coming.*

It was the second time that week.

I tried my best to justify her absence. *Maybe she has papers to grade. Maybe her daughter is sick again. Maybe she . . . forgot.*

I'd stored away excuses for her the same way I stashed bobby pins—putting a few in my car, stowing a few in my purse, never knowing when I might need one. But somehow, just like those bobby pins, the excuses vanished one by one until there weren't any left.

How did we get here? I wondered.

Gina and I were working at the same suburban high school. It was my first year as a teacher and I wasn't worried about making friends because I was so focused on reconciling my feelings of inadequacy as a twenty-one-year-old authority figure for eighteen-year-old students. Between grading, lesson-planning, and administrative tasks, I didn't think I'd have time for friendship.

But soon we were inseparable. She had a lot more classroom experience than I did and the students all respected her. She was cool and self-assured. Everything I wanted to be.

There was just one problem: She canceled plans with me all the time. Like, all. The. Time.

It had become totally normal for us to make plans only for her to cancel minutes before. Twice, she'd been a complete no-show, failing to answer calls and texts with questions about whether she was on her way. The following day, she'd always mention something about losing her phone or falling asleep.

"My bad," she'd offer half-heartedly, and I'd muster yet another, "No, that's cool. I get it!"

But I didn't get it. For some reason, as vocal as I am, I never said anything. Despite my reputation for telling it like it is, I *never addressed* how frustrating it was or how embarrassed I felt when she stood me up. Maybe it's because I didn't want to push away someone I felt lucky enough to be "chosen" by. But it bothered me endlessly.

As I remained silent on the issue, my anger presented itself in other ways. I became increasingly sarcastic when she asked me questions, offering passive-aggressive comments and rolling my eyes whenever I'd overhear her make plans with others. "Yeah, well, that's *if* she shows up, right, Gina?" I'd say with a smirk that I tried to pass off as playful. She had such an "I can take it or leave it" approach, and maybe the heart of the matter was I felt disposable.

Seeing how unfazed she was by the entire situation only angered me more. I often complained to my boyfriend about her lack of consideration, and while he initially tried to give helpful advice, he eventually grew weary of hearing the same story.

"Just tell her, Danielle. Tell her." But didn't he understand that it just wasn't that *simple?*

When I began studying female friendship a few years later, I felt validated to learn that it really *is* complicated. There are so many factors that lead to women's tendencies to remain averse to conflict—especially with friends.

These findings were confirmed by woman after woman who sat across from me during coaching sessions, struggling to explain why she was suppressing her anger instead of expressing it to her friend.

But the issue might be much bigger than us.

Many of us would like to think of ourselves as strong, opinionated women who are unafraid to speak their mind. But there are certain situations (and friendships) that have us biting our tongue more than we'd like. And depending on our background, personality, and general attitude toward conflict, we might have an even greater tendency toward avoidance.

There are three main factors that influence women's decision to circumvent confrontation at all costs: our relationship with anger, gender bias, and people-pleasing. These elements work together to keep us from mustering the courage to address hard issues head on. Because sometimes it just feels like too great a risk.

The Paradox of Anger

When our friends upset us, we often choose to turn our rage inward, stewing as it bubbles into resentment and bitterness. Much of this avoidance has to do with our relationship with anger itself.

In her book *Men, Women, and Aggression*,[35] Anne Campbell writes:

> Women split themselves into two people: the angry self and the responsible self that reigns in the anger. Thus, we're angry with ourselves on two counts: for expressing our anger and for restraining it. . . . Women see aggression as a temporary loss of control caused by overwhelming pressure and resulting in guilt. Men see aggression as a means of exerting control over other people when they feel the need to reclaim power and self-esteem.

When women's anger is viewed as an inconvenient slip, whereas men's is seen as an instrument for respect and resolution, there will be inevitable consequences in our close relationships.

If we see anger as an emotion we need to suppress, we'll fight to hold back during times when we've been legitimately aggrieved. But this is a missed opportunity, because anger is a productive emotion that can inspire us to make our pain known, which gets us one step closer toward both personal and relational healing.

You can probably recall a time when you wanted to blow up at a friend for something but decided to hold it in. In your moment of restraint, you likely calculated the social risks of how your rage might be interpreted, and the guilt you would have felt after you screamed your head off.

Lena was a friend I had in my early twenties who provoked me just as much as she calmed me. We'd shared so much with each other during our time in college—parties, boys, spirituality, shameful indulgences— and our deep familiarity brought with it an unsettling knowledge of what made the other person tick.

One semester, we were both taking a class that required us to go door-to-door together and interview our neighbors. At the last second, my anxiety got the best of me and I made up some excuse about not being able to do it. She was upset that I bailed last minute, and after going back and forth for a bit, she hit me with, "Well, I guess my parents just raised me to be a person who does what they say they're going to do."

I thought, *Did this heffa really just accuse me of not having any home training?*

I don't often have the urge to punch somebody, but, man, I wanted to hit her.

Instead, my eyes filled with tears as I fought to restrain myself, and I stormed into my room. I was mad at her for the insult, but I was mostly pissed at myself, both for backing down and for being angry at all.

Not wanting to make it a "big deal," I didn't even address the incident the next day. I just avoided eye contact until a moment of laughter would distract us from the tension so that I could push myself into believing that nothing really happened and I was overreacting. Because I'm not an angry person. So, it all must've been a misunderstanding. Right?

The culture in your home plays a major role in how you deal with your anger as well. Depending on whether your parents chastised you for "having an attitude" or encouraged you to express your rage as a form of strength, it impacts the choices you make about how to respond when you've been offended.

For some of us, the fear of appearing angry runs so deep that we squirm over expressing anything in the *proximity* of rage. When we've been raised with teachers preaching, "If you don't have anything nice to say, don't say anything at all," words with even the slightest bit of unpleasantness feel like an all-out attack. So, in an effort to avoid having a simple request mis-interpreted as anger, we don't . . . well . . . say "anything at all."

The tolerance for irritation is especially low for Black women, a group already characterized by others as being inherently angry.

It certainly helps when we develop friendships with women who help us to feel safe. I want to know that there's room for not only my celebra-tions and my sorrows, but for my rage, as well. This might be why so many of my Black clients say they feel more open and comfortable with their Black friends (at least initially) compared to non-Black friends. In these spaces, we feel more comfortable "fussing" and expressing anger as an extension of our humanity without pretense, fear, or apology.

For Black women who subscribe to the Strong Black Woman schema[36]—the idea that Black women are emotionally tough and expected to care for everyone around them—they'll experience more mental health con-sequences, such as depression, anxiety, and loneliness. Because of certain cultural stereotypes and ideals, it becomes especially important to be in spaces where our anger is safe—even if that anger is directed (in a healthy way) toward a friend.

It's interesting to see how so many intersecting parts—our race, our upbringing, our cultural influences—determine how and with whom we avoid conflict. If we see anger as contradictory to harmony (as opposed to an emotion that can function to inspire change within the relationship), are we less willing to express anger with friends? Do we feel more com-fortable expressing anger in relationships with men? Do we intuitively know that—because of how women perceive anger—sharing that emo-tion might be risky in a female-dominated space?

Once we can more readily view anger as an alarm that something is wrong and use it to constructively reconcile a perceived injustice, maybe we'll spend less time trying to avoid the very conflicts that could bring us greater understanding and appreciation with the women we love most.

"Just Be Nice"

Although we'd like to think we're aware of and therefore immune to the various gender biases against women, the truth is that in order to maintain certain norms and function "harmoniously" with our peers, we may find ourselves upholding the very ideas we know to be problematic. Sometimes, our willpower simply feels like it's no match for years of conditioning.

The ramifications of perpetuating negative stereotypes of women seem obvious. If we believe women to be catty and dramatic, then we'll be more likely to dismiss opportunities to work through hard things, writing it off with a *"This is why I can't deal with women—too much drama!"*

But it's the *benevolent* stereotypes that play an unsuspecting role in our conflict avoidance. If we believe that women should be likable, loyal, and nurturing, then we'll avoid confrontation in an attempt to maintain these characterizations.

Gender Bias: Women Should Be Loyal

I once coached a therapist named Mandy who was in the middle of a major friendship decision. She'd been best friends with Lynn for more than fifteen years . . . and she was *tired*. Mandy shared example after example of how Lynn could be chronically negative, emotionally explosive, and so judgmental that it made it difficult for Mandy to be vulnerable with her.

"At the risk of oversimplifying things, Mandy," I told her, "you should be able to bring your full self to the table in a friendship. It sounds like you feel such a need to measure your words and withhold your feelings to maintain this . . . ecosystem . . . that you're personally suffering for it."

"You know what? Lynn and I haven't spoken in a few weeks since she blew up at me," Mandy said, "and honestly, I've felt a little...relieved."

She sighed and dropped her shoulders. Mandy was hungry for a life without the friendship that kept her trapped, and yet she stayed.

When I asked Mandy what scared her most about letting go, her eyes filled with tears and she removed her glasses to wipe them away.

"She's done so much for me." She shook her head back and forth. "That woman was there for me during my divorce—she helped with laundry, sat with me, she...was so loyal. What would it say about me if I left?"

This belief can set us up for trouble in our friendships when we fear speaking up (or letting go altogether) will make us look like a "bad friend." If we view loyalty as a staple of womanhood, then we might suppress our real desires so that no one questions our faithfulness.

Gender Bias: Women Should Be Nurturing

Often characterized as the more nurturing gender, women are charged with the expectation of showing gentleness to others. This kind of bias can play a role in how we avoid conflict with friends if we think that confrontation is the opposite of being caring.

A few years back, I was working with a stay-at-home mom who was overwhelmed by a friend's neediness. She was able to manage things at first, but she found her psychological and emotional reserves depleting pretty quickly.

When I asked her why she refused to share her feelings with her friend, she told me about how she struggled to reconcile the idea of saying no with the idea she had of herself as a nurturer.

"I don't want her to think that I don't care about her. Because if I actually say what I want to say, it's gonna look like I'm not in her corner, you know? I don't think she has anyone else to help her, so I'm that person. And I feel like...I don't want that responsibility but that's just what it is."

As an active church member and community volunteer, she endured the burden of this friendship dynamic because the idea of giving pushback felt like something a caring and nurturing woman just wouldn't do.

Gender Bias: Women Should Be Likable

You may often hear about "likeability bias"—an expectation that women be less assertive so as to receive social approval, whereas men are allowed space to speak and think against the grain.

If women subconsciously subscribe to this same double standard, how does it infiltrate their friendships?

When I was a high school teacher, I most looked forward to class discussions around a novel we'd just read. My students were so insightful, and I learned a lot from the diverse perspectives in the room. But it never failed that when discussing female protagonists, much of the students' conversation centered on whether they liked or disliked her. When we analyzed male protagonists, the issue rarely came up.

I've seen this play out in my personal life too. I've definitely found myself sitting among a group of women as they evaluated a new "member" in her absence. There is talk about not liking her "vibe," "attitude," or even the way she walked in the room (I've been criticized for this twice, actually. When confronting an older colleague about why she was always unpleasant with me, she told me, "It's just the way you *walk* in here, like you think you *better* than every damn body!")

For some reason, the critique of unfavorable men is attached to tangible deficiencies: foul things that they said, obvious oversights that they made. But when women are the subjects of those critiques, the feedback feels more elusive. We have to interrogate the ways that our subconscious expectation for women to be likable contributes to us showing up inauthentically.

If we know that any trivial misstep could be reason enough to be rejected by other women, we'll be more likely to avoid conflict, holding back from voicing our needs and calling out bad behavior.

And while a fear of being disliked may be a personal struggle for some more than others, there's no denying that a larger societal expectation of women as likable sometimes permeates the decisions we make within our female friendships.

Gender Bias: Women Should Be Empathetic

A UCLA study[37] found that when watching others in pain, women's brains showed more empathy than men's did. They showed each participant videos of people in pain, and while there were no outwardly noticeable differences in how each sex responded, their neural activity told a different story.

Female participants showed higher activity in parts of the brain associated with pain than did their male counterparts, which means our brain is mimicking what would happen to us if we were in the same situation. Apparently, when we say, "I feel your pain," we mean it.

But I can't help but wonder how this propensity toward empathizing can sometimes work to our detriment.

I'm sure you can recall a time when you wanted to share a tough truth with a friend, but held back, thinking, *I don't want to hurt her feelings.*

You're not alone.

My inbox is filled with essay-style messages from women outlining a friendship dilemma that ends with "but I don't want to make her feel bad." Do we sometimes *over*empathize with a friend's emotions, becoming immobilized by the thought of causing her harm?

Dr. Tracy Alloway is an award-winning psychologist whose work focuses on the female brain. Her book *Think Like a Girl*[38] highlights ways women can harness their unique thinking strengths.

"When women make decisions, they aren't just acting because they're 'emotional'; they're acting because they want to protect. They want to reduce as much harm as possible."

Dr. Alloway explained that ruinous empathy occurs when we overcorrect on our need to protect, and become so focused on others' feelings that it becomes detrimental to our own well-being.

Sometimes the anxiety of just *imagining* how uncomfortable a friend may become in response to raising an issue may be almost just as bad as *seeing* her actual discomfort during a confrontation. Typically, once a woman's mustered the courage to say what she feels, she'll backpedal if her friend looks upset. She'll dilute her message in the form of apologies or minimizing statements like "But...I mean, what do I know? I might just be overthinking it" or "I'm sorry, I could be wrong..."

While we may be neurologically wired to consider a friend's feelings, we're *culturally* conditioned to put those feelings above our own.

Breaking Free from People-Pleasing

I think we intuitively know that it's dangerous to be a woman without any relationships. We wonder about the woman without any friends, looking at her as our greatest fear realized. Do we view the friendless woman as a social pariah? And does a paralyzing fear of sharing her fate drive us to stay in even the unhealthiest of friendships?

I've never identified as a people-pleaser, but I'd worked with enough women to know that it was a tendency that was stopping them from having satisfying friendships. They were tired and resentful and feeling isolated in a trap that they seemed to have created for themselves.

But the fear of conflict outweighed their desire to show up authentically.

Terri Cole is a psychotherapist and relationship expert who I interviewed for my podcast, *Friend Forward*. She's known for her tough-love approach and extensive knowledge on the power and psychology of boundary-setting, and I wanted to include her insights on an episode about people-pleasing.

"Simply put, people-pleasers are those who say yes when they want to say no. But when we tell our friends things that aren't true, we're giving them corrupted information, which leads to a friendship that lacks trust."

In the moments when we anticipate friction, we abandon our real needs and desires and convince ourselves that we're doing it in service of the friendship.

But that excessive self-sacrificing isn't worth it.

Research[39] finds that while both men and women might avoid conflict, men experience a decrease in emotional exhaustion, but the same is not true for women. Conflict avoidance is also associated with more emotional labor for women (because of the emotional work it takes to hide your true feelings) but not for men.

The consequences aren't only internal, they're relational. If you're continually self-abandoning for the sake of your friends' comfort, you will never be fully known. This sets you up for a lifetime of unsatisfying friendships as you grow ever resentful...and less likely to experience platonic intimacy.

Suppressing your emotions means they'll only take longer to dissipate, so the challenge becomes how to name and challenge your anger in a way that motivates positive change for you both individually and relationally for the sake of the friendship.

Taking Inventory of Your Avoidance

To assess the damage of suppressing your issues, ask yourself these questions:

- *Who else is indirectly suffering as a result of my avoiding conflict with a friend?* Do you consistently vent about your friend to other people in your life (e.g., your partner, brother, other friends)? Do other people in your network get less of you (your time, emotions, attention) because of the energy you dedicate to avoiding an open address of concerns with your friend? What are the stealthy ways that this unresolved conflict has seeped into other areas of your life?
- *How is my body responding to the stress?* Have you noticed any trouble sleeping, eating, or concentrating on other tasks? Does your heart race when you get a text from your friend or before you're supposed to meet up with her? Have you been getting headaches or experiencing any other symptoms of your stress? This could be your body's

way of telling you it needs relief from being suspended in a harmful state driven by certain negative emotions.

- *How is my friendship impacted by my decision to avoid conflict?* Sometimes recognizing the impact of your avoidance on the relationship is more difficult to spot. Have you become passive-aggressive or sarcastic to cope with uncomfortable situations? Are you slowly distancing yourself from your friend, leaving her to wonder what's going on? And could your friendship be improved if you actually spoke up?

- *Is this decision to stay quiet in line with my general values about friendship?* Think about the qualities that are important to you. If you value honesty, consider how you can demonstrate that during moments of tension. If support is important to you, think about how you can position yourself to receive the support you deserve by openly communicating your needs to your friend.

Reframing conflict as an opportunity to meet a need instead of as a threat can be the first step toward alleviating yourself from the stress that comes from suppressing your concerns.

Dr. Carole Robin is internationally known for her expertise in interpersonal relations, and she coauthored the book *Connect: Building Exceptional Relationships with Family, Friends, and Colleagues.*[40]

"Women in particular are afraid of how they'll be seen if they raise a 'pinch.' They'll either be seen as being overly sensitive, or dramatic, or thin-skinned, or 'What's the matter with you? Everything's got to be a big thing!'" Dr. Robin warns that not raising things when they're a tiny "pinch" means it'll grow into a "crunch," and make conflict even more intense.

"A lot of people say, 'It's not worth raising it,' but I tell them to try substituting 'I,' 'you,' or 'we.' *I'm* not worth raising it. *You're* not worth raising it. *We*, our relationship, is not worth raising it. Then, ask yourself again whether you want to raise it in service of the relationship."

People pleasers may sometimes struggle with this because they become so attuned to others' needs that the signal often minimizes their own.

We have to figure out a way to release the mental model that conflict damages relationships. Telling a friend that she's doing something problematic is an act of care. It shows that we're invested, otherwise, we wouldn't bother.

And, let's be honest: there's a chance that when you finally do express yourself, it doesn't go well. Maybe your friend gets defensive. Maybe she misunderstands your point. Do not take that as a sign that you should regret speaking up for yourself. The outcome may be less than ideal, but the goal is to honor your integrity by giving voice to your feelings and create an opportunity to get a need met. Your friend then has a choice to accept or reject your invitation. But even her rejection is data, as it informs your decision about how to best invest your time and energy—and with whom.

Remember, the right friends will not be offended by your taking up space. They'll welcome it because they want to *know* you.

But it starts with your believing that you're worth knowing.

Chapter 4 Questions

1. How do you manage feelings of anger, and how has your response been shaped by your upbringing?
2. Have you ever had people-pleasing friends? Describe the relationship with this personality type.
3. How have your ideas about what women "should be" impacted your approach to a recent friendship conflict?

Chapter 5 Preview Question

When you think of "women's aggression," what comes to mind?

Mean Girls

The Art of Relational Aggression (a.k.a. Sophisticated Stealth)

I was scrolling on social media recently when I came across a video of a woman who appeared to be in her midtwenties. She was at a baseball game and had set her phone on a tripod, placed it in front of her seat, and began recording herself making a few cute poses.

There were two girls behind her—who looked to be around the same age—and when they saw the young lady recording herself and noticed the two of them appeared in the background of the influencer's video, they began mocking her. They rolled their eyes behind her, threw up their middle fingers, laughed with condescension, and shouted insults.

The influencer posted the video to social media, highlighting the ways these girls were taunting her at the game. As you can imagine, the video spread like wildfire. Within days, it had accumulated millions of views.

People began posting response videos, calling out the behavior and sharing their own experiences with bullies. Within forty-eight hours, people had discovered the identity of the two girls and began sharing each one's personal information online, which led to a sea of harassment.

The whole thing was pretty intense, but it's not the first time something like that has happened online. With the omnipresence of cell phones and recording devices, it only takes a few seconds for a moment of "mean girl" behavior to be plastered across the internet. The outrage is swift and the event becomes a trending topic as people are prompted to share their own stories of victimization at the hands of cruel women.

We rally almost instinctually because it's an image we've seen one hundred times before. The belligerence of women who taunt and tease others unprovoked is enraging, and we're appalled by their shameless antagonism.

These extreme behaviors are objectively vile. And in the larger conversation around women's anger, *these* are the images we often think of first. But how did "mean girls" like these become the face of women's aggression?

The reality is that we *all* aggress to some degree. It's an impulse critical to survival as we work to protect ourselves and our resources. But when these extremes are the most prolific representation of what it means to be aggressive, we can't see ourselves in that depiction, so we claim to never aggress at all.

But most of us have pulled from the "mean girl" handbook once or twice, especially when we felt we *had* to. And most times it's to protect ourselves... and the women we love most.

The Secret Language of Relational Aggression

The set of behaviors we use to strike at each other has a name: *relational aggression*. It's a form of aggression that often lives "underground," operating covertly to minimize risks to the aggressor. Although men and women both use this type of aggression, open forms of aggression typically come with major social consequences for women more than men, and so they might choose to strike using tactics that are harder to detect.

Four common forms of relational aggression are:

- Gossip
- Silent treatment
- Exclusion
- Public embarrassment

Each one of these tactics targets relationships, likely because relationships are a woman's primary resource. Gossiping about someone taints their reputation and therefore impacts the way that others connect with them; the silent treatment creates distance in a relationship; exclusion cuts people off from relationships; and embarrassing someone publicly can change their relationship with those who witness the humiliation.

This is why we often hear jokes about how men might punch someone when they're upset, but women are engaging in full-out psychological warfare.

Meanness and Motivation

I'd like to think that the average, reasonable woman is not walking around inflicting harm on other people unprovoked. She doesn't have the desire... or the time. Those who delight in bullying others are coming from such an extreme place of pain and viciousness, the stuff nightmares are made of.

But there are those of us who pull from the mean girl toolkit only when we feel we've been backed into a corner and the situation calls for us to play the game.

This game-playing might be expected in the workplace with women we anticipate as competition. But sometimes we get so bogged down in conflict with a friend (especially in friend groups!) that we indulge in some degree of the very behaviors we know to be unproductive and unkind.

There are times when a friend calls us out or lets us down, and our first reaction may *not* be to directly address things with maturity and compassion. So, we gossip about her or gradually exclude her, justifying our behavior because we're:

- desperate for a sense of control in situations where we feel powerless
- trying to balance the scales when we believe we've been unjustly hurt
- unequipped with the skills necessary to have a healthy and open dialogue

- protecting our alliances when we sense they're being threatened
- trying to elevate our status when we feel vulnerable and susceptible

It's important to note that intention makes all the difference. Whenever we intend to hurt someone's feelings, we are using tactics to inflict harm. But just because someone's feelings are hurt doesn't mean a person was being malicious toward them.

Some women fear speaking up for themselves because they're worried about being characterized as mean. But for women who are acting out with the purpose of causing distress, it's a whole other story.

The Handbook of Sophisticated Stealth Tactics

Sometimes relational aggression is easy to spot. Maybe a seventh grader shouts at her classmate during lunch: "You can't sit with us!" and everyone around them can clearly see what's happening.

But there's a craftier, more subtle way to strike out against women—and those with higher emotional intelligence may be better at it.

I call this "sophisticated stealth," and trust me: you know it when you see it.

It helps to learn the "rules" of sophisticated stealth so you can better recognize it when it happens to you.

Rule #1: No matter what, maintain an appearance of cooperation.

From a young age, we learn the virtue of being a "good girl." Many of us are encouraged by everyone from our teachers and parents to be nice and soft spoken. The conditioning runs so deep that when we find ourselves genuinely angry and wanting to fire back at a woman who has hurt or threatened us, we look for undetectable ways to aggress.

If we openly signal to other women that we're hostile, aggressive, and uncooperative, we risk getting cut off from relationships—our number one resource.

The key to sophisticated stealth is to hit your target without looking like the bad guy. During times of conflict with friends, our aggression lives underground; to be found out is to risk isolation.

This might also explain why some of the meanest women you know might also have the highest reputation.

Rule #2: Hit with your words, not your fists.

While men might punch each other to establish dominance, they're expected to express their anger that way. "Boys will be boys," they say. Young girls, therefore, are taught that open displays of aggression belong to men.

If there was a lot of emphasis on being "ladylike" when you were growing up, you were likely discouraged from being too loud, too rough, too direct. Since open shouting, cursing, and hitting seem to violate the feminine ideal, we turn to words—the softer, the better.

Women who are skilled in sophisticated stealth know how to craft veiled insults:

> *"Wow, I didn't know you'd have the courage to wear an outfit like that. Good for you!"*
> *"I wish I could be less uptight about cleanliness, kind of like you."*
> *"You guys are dating? I didn't expect that you would be his type!"*

My southern belles might know this more simply as "Bless her heart."

Rule #3: Deny, deny, deny.

If the first rule of sophisticated stealth is to not be found out, then the words and actions used by the perpetrators will be like carbon monoxide—potent to the target but impossible to touch. This way if they're confronted about their behavior, it becomes easier to deny.

Let's say you've recently fallen out with a friend who's disappointed you one too many times. Each of you thinks the other one's in the wrong, but so far neither of you has offered an apology to mend the relationship. Tensions are running high, and during a mutual friend's birthday party, she sits across the room stewing as you walk in with a few other ladies.

As you make your way into the kitchen, she makes a big show of walking over and greeting everyone else but subtly skips over you. Later, she asks—in front of everyone—about the progress you're making with your job search, a subject she knows you're sensitive to.

You lock eyes with her searching for evidence of remorse, and you notice the faintest outline of a smirk.

When you confront her about her behavior later that day, she denies it. She didn't purposely overlook you when she was hugging people, she tells you—she *just didn't see you.* And when she asked about your job hunt, she assures you that she did that out of genuine concern—she didn't realize you were *so sensitive about it.*

Now you've been framed as an unhinged woman.

And she is a woman who's been falsely accused.

The gaslighting is top tier.

Rule #4: Use gossip to plant seeds of doubt.

There are many reasons a woman might gossip about another woman.

She might feel threatened by the woman she's talking about or is trying to solidify her status in the group. She might fear that—after a falling out with a friend—mutual friends will take the friend's side, leaving her isolated and alone.

So, she might find a way to "warn" others by sharing less-than-favorable information about the woman so that others see her in a bad light. She might hint at promiscuity, question her genuineness, or warn about an unpleasant personality.

And she does this carefully, of course.

If her objective is too obvious, she'll look vindictive. So, she must frame her gossip as a noble act she's doing to alert others. She'll sprinkle in statements like "I'm just telling you because I'm worried about her" or "I'm trying to look out for you," for good measure.

This particular strategy appeals to the "Virtuous Victim Effect."[41] This is a phenomenon whereby people tend to see victims of wrongdoing as more moral than nonvictims who have behaved in an identical way. So, intentionally framing oneself as the victim can be advantageous for one's reputation while simultaneously making the "offender" look bad.

I'll never forget the time when my friend Kim became threatened by a new friendship I'd made. Kim and I used to cowork and go to lunch together, but I'd become intrigued by a new woman and had become less available to her.

We were all in a women's business club meeting one afternoon, and when we were headed to the parking lot, Kim pulled me aside.

"So, you and Brooklyn are getting close . . . ," she started.

"Um, yeah, I guess we've been hanging out a little more. It's fun getting to know her."

"That's great! I'm curious, though. Have you ever had money issues with her?"

"What do you mean?" I knew Kim was setting me up for some gossip, but I was trying to pretend I didn't see right through her game plan.

"Well, Megan told me that Brooklyn never paid her half of the retreat, and a few other people were talking about how she's not paying her invoices. I just didn't know if she's tried to pull any of that on you!"

"Oh, wow. Um, no, I don't think so. And if she did, Kim, you know I'd feel very comfortable calling her out on it to her face."

"I know, I know! I'm just looking out for you, you know that."

"Yeah, of course. I appreciate that."

"So, are we still going to lunch tomorrow? Or . . . are you going to be with your new *friend* . . . ?"

Kim packaged her gossip as a concern to get me to change my relationship with Brooklyn and to position herself as a friend who was just doing her honorable duty.

While women *do* share information about others from a *genuine* place of concern, there are other times this behavior is a tactic of sophisticated stealth. But that's exactly why this tactic is so effective: they're banking on people not being able to tell the difference between the two.

Rule #5: When you can, involve third parties.

Sometimes, the relationship a woman uses to cause harm is the relationship with herself. She may use the silent treatment, ignoring her friend in ways that make her feel invisible. Worthless.

But other forms of sophisticated stealth rely on third-party witnesses to be effective.

This could look like "playfully" teasing her in front of an audience, because the impact of the humiliation is dependent on others watching it play out. The "third-party" rule could also take the form of sharing unfavorable information about her target to others to damage their relationship with the subject.

And acts of exclusion are almost entirely dependent on groups of three or more so that the victim feels like an outsider, which causes great emotional distress.

How to Deprogram Your Mind

When we're feeling threatened and insecure, we must remain aware of our tendency to lean in to these behaviors. For some of us, it can feel as if we're working against software that's been downloaded in our mind and reinforced by everyone from family members to society at large.

On a broader scale, we need to destroy patriarchal systems that frame women as petty and hysterical for addressing things directly and assertively. When we're scared that we'll be punished for our anger, we'll either suppress it to avoid conflict altogether or watch as our rage manifests in dysfunctional, passive-aggressive ways.

So many of our decisions are motivated by a fear of being characterized as those very things, and we do what we can to avoid being labeled unfairly—denied permission to operate in the fullness of our humanity.

To reprogram our mind, we must continually ask ourselves the following questions when we're tempted to use these "mean girl" tactics (no matter how justified we feel in the moment).

Questions to ask before saying negative things about a friend to others

- What's my actual objective?
- Do I want others to see her in the same negative light that I do right now or am I just processing with others how I feel?
- Am I seeking support on my journey toward reconciling with my friend?

Let's keep it real: Sometimes when we're sharing factual information about a falling-out with a friend, it's not going to be positive. If we're talking about how annoying it is that she constantly cancels plans to be with her boyfriend, that's not necessarily vicious. But we have to ask ourselves whether we're talking *about* her or *against* her. Then, we have to check ourselves to see whether any part of our sharing is intended to harm her reputation by framing her as the "bad guy" and ourselves as the "good guy" or victim.

Questions to ask before giving her the silent treatment

- Am I doing this because I'm not sure how to articulate my feelings?
- Am I giving her the cold shoulder in an attempt to punish her?
- Do I take pleasure in knowing my friend is likely agonizing over my withdrawal? If so, why?

After a tense misunderstanding with a friend, you might find yourself feeling emotionally distant and that manifests as fewer texts, shorter conversations, and less playfulness. This shift is natural when we're feeling disconnected.

The problem occurs when there's a lack of communication. You may not be ready to talk through your issue or you might be feeling so bothered by her that you don't want to share space. But communicating what's happening makes all the difference. Telling her that you need space or that you are a little upset is a healthy way to give voice to your feelings and validates her concerns that you're pulling away without pretending everything's cool when it's not.

If there's any part of you that's intentionally acting distant because you *want* her to feel bad, you are punishing her. True friendship does not delight in the other person's discomfort. Not only is this relationally aggressive; it's a form of emotional manipulation. Giving the silent treatment and playing games is meant to inflict psychological distress, something we shouldn't want to do to a woman we claim to care for.

Questions to ask before excluding her

- Am I excluding her because I want her to feel like an outsider or because I'm genuinely having a gathering for a specific group of people?
- What are the potential ways that excluding this person could backfire?
- How have I felt when other women intentionally excluded me?

There are many ways that we can exclude a friend during times of conflict. We can host social gatherings that we don't invite her to, or we can exclude her from the group chat, looking for ways to restrict her access to ourselves and to others. Either way, we continue to employ this tactic because it's effective in meeting our objective of keeping her out.

Research by Ginette C. Blackhart reveals that women report higher levels of distress[42] when experiencing social exclusion, and the pain they feel is comparable to that of physical pain.[43] Women also employ social exclusion more than men, and the prevalence of this tactic is probably why women are better able to perceive cues[44] that both predict and interpret when social exclusion is taking place.

When we find ourselves in a weird season with a friend, we tend to create physical distance representative of the emotional disconnection that we feel. There's so much vulnerability involved in communicating how we really feel, so we opt for subtle indirect ways to express our rage, anxiety, and disappointment. And though excluding someone might offer temporary relief, the residual pain of being left out makes it harder to reconcile later.

Insulating Yourself from Relational Aggression

Many of us tolerate relational aggression because it seems so much better than the alternative: being a woman without connections. We'd rather endure emotional assault than be alone.

This kind of approach to conflict continues to fester in some friendships because we've written it off as "women being women," as if the eye-rolling, gaslighting, and gossiping is inherent. But it's something we can take control of if we become aware and then hold each other accountable.

So, how do you respond when a friend begins to use relational aggression during a conflict?

First, try calling it out. Be sure to point to facts instead of observations. Instead of saying, "It seems like you're distant," try "We're not doing our daily check-ins anymore. Is everything okay?" If she responds by telling you that nothing's wrong, take her at her word. As a grown woman, it is her responsibility to voice any concerns that she has. It is not your job to beg, analyze, or decode.

Depending on the situation, it might be best to overlook the aggression altogether. Sometimes the intended impact of relational aggression depends on you *knowing* you weren't invited or actively *registering* that someone's being short with you. Pretending to be oblivious can weaken her attempts to get under your skin. If she hits you with "Wow, I think you're the only person I know who could pull off a skirt that short," say "Thank you!" and refuse to engage with the attack.

You can also anticipate the reaction she wants you to have and commit to not giving it to her. Pretending to be completely oblivious to her passive-aggressiveness or any silent "mean girl cues" she's trying to send your way minimizes the impact she's trying to have on you.

You could also try withdrawing from group dynamics, if possible. For most relationally aggressive tactics to work, a third party is required (e.g., gossip, exclusion). If you notice a shift in the group dynamics, remove yourself from those settings and opt instead to do one-on-ones to preserve your independent friendships and to avoid being in a position where relational aggression can run rampant.

Finally, identify the things you can control. As soon as you get clear about what's your responsibility and what isn't, it can prevent you from ruminating about your friend's tactics. Only put energy toward the things you can control instead of stressing about how to make your friend stop her behavior or fretting about what she's saying behind your back.

While we've all been guilty of less than desirable behavior, you should never tolerate a friend who regularly operates this way. If the behavior continues, call it out directly and tell her you don't appreciate it. Maybe she'll end it, embarrassed that she's been found out. But if she digs her heels in and continues, you may need to end the relationship, because true friends do not take pleasure in another friend's distress.

Disagreements with our girlfriends are inevitable. When women come together, we bring our respective baggage, opinions, and sensitivities— it's only a matter of time before those differences surface and clash. We should forgive a friend who makes mistakes instead of jumping into finding ways to retaliate.

Because these are the moments that test our resolve and block us from healing the fractures in our friendships with vulnerability and healthy communication.

Chapter 5 Questions

1. Recall a time when you were a victim of sophisticated stealth. How did you respond?

2. Have you ever used these tactics during a moment of anger, insecurity, or fear?

3. Were you ever encouraged (directly or indirectly) to use relational aggression as a young girl?

Part 2 Preview Question

Now that you can identify unhealthy approaches to conflict, how confident are you in your ability to know the *right* things to say during times of conflict?

Part Two

WHAT'S REALLY GOING ON

The Art of Understanding

One day, I was sitting on the back patio with a longtime friend, and we were playing catch-up after a few weeks of not seeing each other.

At one point, I segued to a new topic.

"Oh, I have to give you the update on Nadia..."

"Wait, the clingy friend?"

"Um, yeah...her."

I felt a ping of guilt.

Nadia was a newer friend who I really enjoyed, but she'd become increasingly...attached. I found myself overwhelmed by the frequency of her texts and the demands on my time, despite my efforts to be as responsive as I could.

But hearing her referred to as the "clingy friend" got me thinking...

When we first become friends with someone, we get excited by the possibilities of all the relationship might be. But, sometimes, a conflict comes between us and it grows so big that we can't see our friend for all of who she is.

We reduce her to the issue she presents, and before we know it, she becomes "the negative friend," "the clingy friend," "the flaky friend"—but there may be more to the picture than we realize, and failing to recognize the fullness of the situation can negatively impact our friendships.

In Part 1, we learned about the mechanics of female friendship. And while it's important to understand our friendships on a high level, we also need to be equipped with knowledge to tangibly navigate the real day-to-day business of being friends.

When you notice something about a friend that turns you off, it's a big moment. This is because your **interpretation** of events determines your **behavior**, and those things together can alter the trajectory of your friendship.

So, Part 2 is a handbook to help you assess and interpret your friend's "issue" with more warmth and compassion, while also equipping you with scripts and strategies to help you thoughtfully determine how to respond.

Here, you'll find the nine most common "friend types" that take shape during seasons of conflict, and insights to help you through your disconnection.

In each section, you will find:

- A real scenario that offers an operating illustration of the conflict
- A behind-the-scenes breakdown of the scenario to help you approach friends with greater compassion and perspective
- Scripts and strategies to help you know exactly what to say and do
- Signs to know it's time to walk away
- Signs of whether *you're* the problem

Although you might be tempted to skip to the parts that are most applicable to you at this time, I strongly encourage you to read through each of the "friend types." There are overlapping insights that might weave together to paint a larger picture of things you're experiencing in your friendships.

The ultimate goal of this handbook is to remind you of your friend's humanity, and to equip you with ways to reframe your situation: it's not you versus your friend, it's you and your friend against the issue.

Keep this handbook close as you grow into deep friendship with the women around you. Because if some of these issues don't currently apply in this particular season of your life, trust me, it's only a matter of time.

But the good news is, you'll be ready.

The Flaky Friend

You've been looking forward to this for a while, and it's hard to believe that it's finally happening.

Tomorrow, you and a few friends are going on a much-needed road trip, and you couldn't be more excited. Your bags are packed, the playlists are ready, and the backseat is filled with snacks. This is about to be one of the best weeks you've had in a long, long time. You can feel it.

As you head to bed filled with anticipation, your phone dings. You roll your eyes playfully, thinking that it's probably Brianna texting to ask—for the third time—how many outfits is too many for a one-week road trip.

But when you look at the screen, you see that it's not Brianna; it's Julianna.

Sadly, you know exactly what's about to happen:

Don't hate me, but I don't think I can go. I just have a lot going on right now and don't think it would be smart for me to join you two on the trip. I'm sorry! I'll make it up to you when you get back. Have fun!

If this were the first time she'd bailed on plans at the last minute, you'd be a little more understanding. But it's become the norm.

Just last week, she backed out of your standing coffee date.

The reason? She was having a bad hair day.

The truth is, you love everything about Julianna—except her flakiness. It's hard to depend on her, and each time she backs out of plans, you feel more foolish than the last. And while you initially tried to suppress your frustration with mantras like *Everyone has their flaws*, you're beginning to wonder if this is a flaw you're willing to tolerate. It's starting to feel as if she is taking advantage of you, or that she simply isn't feeling the friendship as much as you are. Are you more invested in the relationship, or are you making a big deal out of nothing?

But it doesn't feel like "nothing"; it's a series of disappointments, and you're kind of over it.

How can you keep a friendship with someone who's always letting you down?

Know the Signs

Here are a few signs that you might be dealing with a flaky friend:

- You don't feel confident in her assurances when she agrees to do something.
- She's not the first person you'd call if you needed help with a time-sensitive matter.
- It's difficult to make solid plans because there's a good chance they'll fall through.
- When she announces a new venture, commitment, or interest, you're skeptical about how long it will last.

Getting Perspective

One form of inconsistency that tends to have a negative impact on our friendships is *inconsistently showing up.*

While some may see it as a harmless quirk (*"You know I'm forgetful . . . !"*) or a serious aversion (*"I just don't like to be forced to commit to plans . . ."*), the reality is that it frustrates friends who find themselves on the receiving end.

And here's the thing: lack of follow-through is about so much more than forgetfulness and a noncommittal attitude—in friendship, it's a matter of trust.

Typically, when we talk about trust in friendship, we're referring to someone's vow to not betray us by telling our business, taking advantage of our vulnerability, or making friends with the girl they know we can't stand (kidding...kind of).

But it's also about her willingness to keep her word.

One of the ways that emotional safety is established in a friendship is when we give our friends evidence that they can count on us, and it's achieved by demonstrating reliability consistently over time.

Backing out of commitments and breaking promises is the quickest way to upend any sense of security within the relationship, and people are less likely to believe that you'll be there for them when they need you.

To gain a broader understanding of the factors at play, let's explore reasons that we may find ourselves dealing with a flaky friend.

Possibility 1. There are a host of behind-the-scenes barriers.

I've coached enough women to know that what sometimes manifests as lateness, cancellations, and inconsistency, could be the result of personal issues that someone is working through.

Adults with ADHD will experience forgetfulness[45] and impulsivity, two traits that may make it difficult to follow through with plans. (Let me be clear: it's **not** an excuse to be unreliable, but it is a very real challenge that some have to face as they go about navigating their day-to-day lives.)

Also, those with social anxiety tend to fear interactions with others, which could account for any plans they cancel that involve friends of yours they either haven't met or don't know well. They may accept invitations but change their mind as the time grows nearer, too anxious to face the reality of interacting with others.

A lack of organizational skills can impact the way a friend manages her time and keeps track of her tasks and responsibilities, which could make her more inclined to miss deadlines and not follow through with plans.

While none of these issues is an excuse to flake on friends, it can help to see that her behavior is not motivated by a lack of interest in or respect for you. Knowing this can help you to be more empathetic to challenges she faces as she works to maintain healthy friendships, and it can inform your decisions about how to get your needs met while also honoring her limitations.

Possibility 2. She is not as dedicated to the friendship as you are.

This may be difficult to hear, but *one* reason a friend is consistently unreliable may be that she lacks commitment to (and respect) for the friendship.

And even though this is the part where we typically begin to vilify her for being selfish and inconsiderate, remember that she has a right to choose which relationships she wants to invest in and prioritize.

What she *cannot* do, however, is violate the universal principles of keeping your word and respecting others' boundaries. If you determine that her behavior is a reflection of her apathy for the friendship itself, *you* get to decide whether that extends beyond what you're willing to accept in your friendships. (See "When to Let Go," page 103.)

Possibility 3. She doesn't realize that this matters to you.

Let me tell you: if I had a dollar for every time a client said, "But I shouldn't have to *tell* her this thing bothers me—she should know!" I'd be writing this book from my private luxury estate in Bora-Bora.

Remember, our friendships will never transcend a fundamental need to communicate. If you haven't explicitly stated the way that a friend's inconsistency makes you feel inconvenienced, anxious, and taken advantage of, she honestly might not know that it bothers you.

If people in her life have reduced her chronic unreliability to a cute "quirk" instead of an inconsiderate and irresponsible behavior, she may not believe it to be an actual problem. Consider the messages she has (or has not) received about her lack of consistency and whether there have ever been any consequences in her relationships. If, when she cancels, she hears, "That's okay, no worries!" or she's excused with comments like, "That's so you! I knew you'd cancel," then her lack of follow-through may not be a big deal to her.

What to Do

Once you've gained a bit of perspective to help you approach your friend with compassion, consider the following strategies.

Response 1. Map out the cause and effect.

Sometimes it's easy to minimize our problematic behavior when we don't realize the extent of the impact it has on others. If your friend has a tendency to back out of plans at the last minute, she may genuinely believe that it's not that big of a deal. She may dismiss it, thinking, *Well, there are other people there; I'm sure I won't be missed.*

It's possible that she may not realize her decision affects you that much. So, you'll have to make it plain.

When she cancels, does it alter the night's events? Does it make you upset that you could have spent your time doing something else? What are the costs that come with her decision to pull out? Communicate the actual financial, emotional, and logistical impact of her decision to help her realize the ripple effects of her unreliability.

Try this:

"Hey, I shifted a lot of things around to make time for us to hang out tonight. I was really looking forward to seeing you."

Response 2. Use psychological principles to make her commit.

Robert Cialdini is a professor of psychology who's known as the master of persuasion. In his best-selling book *Influence,*[46] he shares a study conducted at a restaurant in Chicago. Here's what happened:

The restaurant hosts confirmed reservations with guests on the phone using the phrase "Please call if you have to change or cancel your reservation." Despite being asked to call, people still weren't showing up... until the staff tried rephrasing the request.

Instead of telling guests to call if they wanted to cancel, the hosts posed this question instead:

"If you have to change or cancel your reservation, will you call?" Then, they'd wait for the person on the phone to give a clear "Yes."

By the staff's requiring people who were making a reservation to verbalize their commitment to it, the number of no-shows decreased significantly. Asking them to voice their yes made them more likely to follow through.

The same principle can apply with unreliable friends.

You may not be able to change her deep-rooted flaking habit, but perhaps you can at least decrease the frequency of its happening with you.

Try this:

The next time you're planning something and need her to commit, verbalize the specific need and follow it with, *"If you change your mind about coming to the event, can you at least let me know by [deadline]?"* Then, wait for her to say *yes.* (Bonus points if you get her to say yes in front of a few witnesses!)

Response 3. Ask for an explanation.

The next time you're talking to your friend, get curious. Ask her about her patterns and tendencies (in an attempt to genuinely understand, not to accuse).

Try this:

"When I asked you about [event/ activity] you said you'd be there. But now you're saying [contradiction]. What's going on?"

or

"Whenever we have weekend plans it seems like you're regularly unable to commit. What would help us to get more solid plans so things aren't changing at the last minute?"

Remember, if the goal of addressing conflict is to create an understanding (and by extension, deepen our relationships), you cannot approach this from an accusatory place. Getting curious about why she doesn't follow through may give you a new perspective that helps you to better relate to her and adjust accordingly.

When to Let Go

When I work with clients who share frustration about a friend who fails to show up for them, there is obvious resentment (and sometimes contempt). Although some are able to resolve their issues with a willing friend, others realize that they're completely turned off by what they perceive as a lack of consideration, so they stop initiating things and gradually withdraw from the friendship.

Deciding to end a friendship is not necessarily about the faults of the other person; it's more about the unmet needs of the one leaving. Being "flaky" might be a behavior that your friend isn't able to manage, but you get to decide whether it's something you're willing to accommodate. If it's a pattern that can make you lose faith in her, it can be hard when one of the most defining markers of a friendship is having someone you can count on. If you can't help but be frustrated by her perpetual inconsistency (or if you interpret it as disrespect) and no changes have been made after voicing your concerns, consider modifying your expectations or releasing the friendship altogether.

How to Know Whether You're the Flaky Friend

If your friends often make jokes or passive-aggressive comments about not knowing whether you'll show up to something you committed to, it's safe to guess that they may view you as the "flaky friend." Sure, they may have responded with "No worries!" to every cancellation you've thrown their way, but that doesn't mean it hasn't impacted their trust in your ability to show up.

You may also want to consider your general attitude toward the concept of commitment in friendship. Do you believe that one of the main *benefits* of friendship is not having to commit? Do you think friends should be understanding when we change our mind (and do you take full advantage of that)? Are you uncomfortable when people try to pin you down with plans because it feels restrictive?

Sometimes, there are other factors that contribute to your inconsistency—you may be struggling with your mental health or dealing with unpredictable life issues that make it hard for you to know what life will look like from day to day.

To the extent that you feel comfortable, tell your friends why it's hard for you to commit in this season. It gives the context they need to know that, if you don't show up, it's not a reflection of how much you care, but that you are doing your best to manage other behind-the-scenes challenges. Communication really does bridge the gap between ambiguity and understanding.

It's also helpful to ask yourself whether canceling is the exception or the rule. Things happen, and hopefully we have friends who understand that. But if it's the default for how we operate, we might want to reevaluate our approach.

If you attribute your inconsistency to having a more spontaneous, go-with-the-flow approach to life, think about the ways your behavior impacts your friendships. Some of your girls might take it personally; others may not be bothered at all!

When friends ask you to go somewhere and you aren't able, willing, or interested, be very clear from the beginning.

Try this:

"Oh, I'm not going to be able to make it. But call me on Monday and let me know how it went!"

While your friends may be disappointed because they love you and want your company, at least they'll have respect for your directness (and boundary-setting!).

But if you do tell friends that you'll show up for them, honor your commitments, to keep the relationships strong.

The Friend Who Doesn't Reciprocate

Pushing your cart down Target's housewares aisle, you spot a cute mug with a phrase that makes you chuckle to yourself.

Tasha instantly comes to mind. You know she'll find it just as hilarious, so you reach for your phone to snap a picture of the mug and send it to her. But just before you hit Send, you hesitate...

You're *always* initiating texts with Tasha. Why is it that you're the one who has to reach out first when organizing a happy hour, asking for a phone catch-up, or coordinating a playdate?

The whole thing is a bit confusing, because whenever the two of you are together, it's a good time. You have no doubt that she enjoys your company, and you two have a real chemistry. But if that's the case, why does it feel so one-sided?

Admittedly, you hate feeling like you're keeping score, but lately you've noticed that the scales aren't balanced. Lord knows, you don't want to be a bother, but you're beginning to wonder whether you look desperate for always reaching out first.

If you're the one who's doing the work to keep momentum in the friendship, does it mean that she's simply not as invested as you are?

Should you give up on a friend who's not matching your effort, or is it possible to meet in the middle?

Know the Signs

Here a few signs that you may be experiencing a lack of reciprocity in your friendship:

- Your friend's tendency to take doesn't match her willingness to give.

- You've begun scorekeeping, concerned about who gives what (and how much).
- You're beginning to feel foolish because it feels like you're being taken advantage of.
- You're beginning to feel unappreciated.
- Your friend seems oblivious to how much work you're putting into the relationship.
- You fear that you prioritize the friendship more than your friend does.

Maintaining Perspective

If I had to rank the friendship issues that women bring to my office, "lack of reciprocity" would easily be in the top three. I've found that it's at the heart of several other friendship conflicts, and it forces us to more closely examine what we truly require in a friendship.

Typically, the lack of balance is about our time, energy, feelings, or resources. Whenever we sense that we are giving more than we're getting, it registers as a violation of an unspoken agreement to contribute equally to the friendship.

But this collective complaint about reciprocity doesn't just mean that there are women out here who simply aren't pulling their weight in their friendships (although there are). I've found that it points to something deeper.

In romantic partnerships, women tend to carry the majority of the mental and emotional labor. (And while this is not okay, many of us still work to meet that expectation.) In our jobs, we are saddled with "office housework"[47]—lower-level, less-technical tasks—even despite having achieved partner or executive status. As mothers, we give selflessly and sacrificially to our children without expectation. In nearly every space we occupy, we are often expected to bear the weight.

With this as our reality, we look to friendship as our refuge, a space free from those power dynamics. We expect a mutual pursuit and an equal relationship.

Reciprocity is a universal virtue, but it is especially important within female friendship because women live in a world that often takes so much from us.

Before you begin to question whether you should keep reaching out (and start growing resentful!) with a friend who seems less invested, take a step back and consider all the factors that might be in play.

Possibility 1. She has other commitments that take precedence in this season of her life.

Whether it's career advancement, caring for young children, or tending to aging parents, other things that require your friend's attention may indirectly impact you. She has only so much time and attention she can give, and depending on the other demands in her life, you may receive very little of both.

This doesn't mean it's personal. Nor does it speak to your worth.

What she's giving to you may not be reflective of how much she cares for you, but rather of her capacity. It can be a matter of logistics: it's just not possible to consistently commit the same amount of time and energy to everyone we care for. We are constantly negotiating how to spend our time—a limited resource. If you haven't been ranking high on her priority list lately, consider the weight of the other things she may be carrying.

Her lack of reciprocity may be less about *your not* being chosen, and more about her choosing the most urgent matter at hand. It's not an active decision, but a natural consequence of her investing elsewhere.

If this imbalance is new, then extend grace by getting curious about the other priorities in her life that may be requiring more of her than usual.

Possibility 2. She's not aware of certain social norms.

One of the things we often glorify about female friendship is the "unspoken language" we seem to share. But the reality is that some women have never learned it. You might think it's obvious for your friend to reciprocate in a certain way, but she may not know that.

If you are friends with someone who is neurodivergent, for example, she may not reciprocate in the ways you're hoping for. You might think it's "obvious" that she know what to say when you need emotional support or that she know to check in or offer a certain level of focus or attention, but some women will not know those things without your making it plain.

A recent *New York Times* feature[48] shared data that reveals autistic girls are typically underdiagnosed, with many women being diagnosed later in life. This is likely because the symptoms don't always present in the ways people might expect them to.

Consider the possibility that your friend's lack of reciprocity may not necessarily be due to a lack of investment in or care for the friendship, but to broader issues that speak more to her awareness and abilities.

Possibility 3. She fears rejection.

I can't tell you how many women I've spoken to who say they'd be more active in their friendships if they had less fear:

Fear that voicing their needs will be burdensome

Fear that suggesting a night on the town will inconvenience their friends

Fear that saying they want more will make them look clingy or demanding

Fear that they won't have the time, energy, or capacity to sustain a relationship, so they don't give fully or consistently of themselves

Even if, over the course of your friendship, there's been mounting evidence of your mutual affection and concern for each other, your friend may still have these thoughts. And they may hold her back from showing up in the way that she'd like. Consider this during the times you are tempted to call her selfish and pull away without explanation.

Possibility 4. You have different ideas of reciprocity.

In a perfect world, you'd never have to tell a friend that you wish she'd give/do/say/show up more. She would immediately sense your dissatisfaction and make the necessary changes. Or you'd be so in sync that your telepathic powers would keep you in continuous harmony, not a single inequality to be found.

But the truth is, reciprocity doesn't work that way. Sometimes, reciprocity can be elusive . . . and relative. You have a vantage point that allows you to see all the ways in which you contribute to your friendship. But you have less access to your friend's. Do you both share the same definition of reciprocity?

It's possible that your friend doesn't experience the relationship as one-sided. From her perspective, there may be a healthy balance in what both of you are giving: While you may initiate hangouts, she may offer to give you a ride and show up enthusiastically. While you may be looking for more balance in the area of vulnerability, she may think that—while she doesn't share as much as you—she's contributing by listening consistently and attentively whenever you open up.

Get clear on the ways you'd like her to reciprocate and compare them with the ways she's actually showing up. If there's a discrepancy that you aren't satisfied with, it may be time for you to verbalize your needs.

Possibility 5. You value the friendship more than she does.

A study[49] suggests that only half of our friendships are reciprocal. This doesn't mean that half of your friends like you while the other half don't. It means that while you rank someone as your number one girl, she may rank you as her number four.

This isn't personal, it's logistical. Because of the unique way that her social network has been constructed over the course of her life, you may not fall on each other's "hierarchies" in the same way.

I see this play out most often in bridal parties. Several brides-to-be and would-be maids of honor seek coaching for the sensitive dilemma of bridal party selection. There's tension when one friend assumes she'll be asked to be a bridesmaid but realizes the bride has no intention of asking her. Brides come to me with tearful pleas to help them figure out how to choose, and then, how to deliver the news to those they won't include.

It's awkward because you spend your entire friendship under the assumption that you rank each other equally, but weddings force us to put our friendship rankings on public display, and this can be incredibly difficult for the women involved (and the reasons that many opt out of bridal parties altogether). Once things are decided, it's difficult for some friends to recover, believing the other's true feelings have been exposed.

It's hard to accept that your friend may not "rank" you in the same way. But to put things in perspective, consider things the other way around. Are there women in your life who consistently show up for you and have demonstrated a major interest, with whom you do not share the same feelings? It doesn't make them any less wonderful, but you just have other women you prioritize above them—it's rarely personal.

If your friend doesn't seem to value your relationship in the same way, it doesn't mean that you are any less valuable. And learning this truth doesn't have to be discouraging; it can be liberating. This means that you can give without expectation, love with monitoring, and pursue without measuring—not withholding until things are even but, instead, giving freely because you *want* to.

Show up for her because you want to, finding a way to appreciate the value she adds to your life.

What to Do

After you gain a bit of perspective on the matter, it's time to think about how you want to respond.

Response 1. Make your desire known.

If there's a discrepancy between what you're getting and what you want, you have to make it known. Sometimes, you're going to have to put words to what you're feeling.

Is it possible that your friend would show up in the ways you're looking for if she had access to all the information that you do?

Consider the ways she *does* contribute to the relationship, and then get clear on exactly what it is you need. Then, muster the courage to make it known.

Try this:

"I know that I'm the main one who suggests that we go to brunch, but I'm sure there are ideas that you've been sitting on for what you'd like us to do together. Do you want to think about what we're doing next weekend and get back to me?"

This approach *invites*; it doesn't *accuse*, which you'll want to avoid at all costs. Find ways to verbalize that you'd like more balance and that you're willing to work with her to achieve it.

You can also try this:

"I notice that I share things about my life with you, and I may be making things one-sided. I know balance is important, so I hope you know how eager I am to learn more about your life too. How do you feel about [subject you'd like to know more about]?"

This approach assumes that she's not intentionally withholding and communicates a desire for her to lean in to balancing the friendship.

You can also try:

"I'd love for you to [action you want to see more of] more. How can we make that happen?"

This approach is more direct, while it positions your request as something you're willing to solve collaboratively. It also decreases the chances for misunderstanding about how you feel, and shows her that your purpose in sharing is not to push her away but to experience more of her.

Response 2. Adjust your expectations.

This can sound a lot like "just settle." But the two phrases are not synonymous. Whereas one tells us to neglect our needs and find a way to be satisfied with that which doesn't fill us up, the other encourages us to get creative about our path to joy.

Adjusting your expectations with a friend who's not reciprocating means getting real about her willingness and capacity to contribute in the way that you'd prefer. Once you've assessed what's possible, see whether you can find other aspects of the friendship to enjoy and appreciate.

Maybe you're disappointed that she doesn't initiate get-togethers, but she's always the first to comment on your posts. Everybody needs a hype woman!

Or perhaps she doesn't text back as frequently as you'd like, but she makes you belly laugh every time you're together. It's nice to have someone who gets your sense of humor.

If you can zero in on the ways she does add value to the relationship and release her from your expectations of *more*, then you may find a way to be less frustrated with (and even more appreciative of?) her role in your life.

Response 3. Take stock of your friendship inventory.

It's hard not to fixate on what you're not getting from your friend. But what if you shifted your focus?

Is it possible that while you've been working to feel appreciated by one friend, a whole host of friends have been showing you the care and attention you desire? Turn your attention to those women in your life who have been calling, the ones who have responded to every social media post and who regularly suggest that you two get together. Consider opening up to them, returning their interest, and exploring the possibilities of going deeper with them to feel a sense of reciprocity that you've been lacking elsewhere.

When to Let Go

Before you completely end the friendship, consider this:

In what ways would you like her to contribute to the friendship? What action could she be taking to make you feel like things are more balanced, and is she aware? How long have you been feeling that things aren't balanced between you? What areas do you feel that you're giving more than she is?

You'll also want to look out for the following indicators that it's time to release the relationship:

- No matter how hard you try, you can't find a way to adjust your expectations.
- She consistently makes promises of meeting your expectations, but has shown little to no effort.
- She seems to be happily taking but unwilling to give.
- She makes you feel that what you want from her is unreasonable, not possible.
- The imbalance seems intentional on her end (transactional).

If the lack of reciprocity has been happening for a while and hasn't improved in spite of attempts to create more balance, then you may determine that you no longer want to invest in something that doesn't have a good return.

Once you let go, it's important to remember this: If someone does not show the same effort and enthusiasm, it is not a reflection of your worth as a friend. You may be tempted to question why you weren't interesting enough, funny enough, or lovable enough for her to pursue you in the same way you did for her. But your value is not determined by her actions (or inactions). Remain confident in who you are and what you have to offer as a friend.

How to Know Whether You're the Friend
Who Doesn't Reciprocate

If you tend to wait for others to initiate hangouts and they are often the ones to call, check in, and invite more than you do, it's possible they might perceive an imbalance in the relationship.

You may also examine some of your attitudes toward friendship in general. If you believe that friendship is something you'll get to after everything else in your life is situated, then you're not prioritizing it. This may show up in your lack of effort to keep things balanced with your friends.

Also, consider how often you say that "friendship should be easy." If you subscribe to the idea that everything should unfold organically, you're less likely to be intentional about showing up for your friends. Rethink the time and effort you put toward your platonic relationships, and whether the women in your life could say, with confidence, that you care just as much as they do.

Reciprocity is relative, so it's possible that you're giving all you can in the way that feels comfortable to you and you have friends who want more. If this is the case, it could be helpful to: communicate your friendship style to align expectations, explicitly ask your friends how satisfied they are with the friendship and if there's anything you could be doing better, or focus on friendships where your outreach and giving style is more compatible.

The "Gossip"

You're at brunch with a new group of friends when, less than five minutes in, they begin talking about a woman you all know from your book club.

"I didn't realize that she came from money," one says. "I mean, she's great, don't get me wrong—I love Layla. It just...puts things in perspective."

The ladies begin to murmur, adding their own commentary to the story. One leans in, lowers her voice, and whispers, "I always wondered, because I know that her job at the agency can't possibly pay for all that she has going on: the clothes, that apartment...It just never made sense to me. But *now* I understand."

"Do you think her parents are funding the new business too?"

She's asking *you*.

You freeze, completely at a loss for words. Typically, you don't chime in on matters about other people's business, but you know that there's an expectation for you to share your thoughts. So, you flag down the waiter to order another mimosa in hopes that it buys you some time.

How are you supposed to respond? If you confess that you don't want to join in, they'll think you're self-righteous. But if you add your speculations about Layla and her financial situation, you'll feel bad about speaking poorly of her.

So what do you do? The gossip makes you a little uncomfortable, but will shutting it down make you look disloyal to the group? Will you look like you're choosing a side by contributing to their catty speculations?

And the biggest question of all...do you even have the right to call it out if you have been guilty of gossiping yourself?

Know the Signs

Here are a few signs that you are dealing with a gossipy friend:

- Most of her conversations involve speculation about someone who's not present.
- Others "joke" about her always being in the know or having the latest "scoop."
- You find yourself feeling nervous before (or after) sharing personal information with her.
- You don't trust her to keep your secrets.

Getting Perspective

I once posted a question on my social media asking women about their "new friend red flags"—the things that new acquaintances do that turn us off.

Hundreds of women weighed in.

The number one response? Gossip.

I wasn't surprised at all. When we meet a new woman and witness her disparage another woman, it makes us uneasy. We become outraged by her recklessness, put off by her disloyalty, and suspicious of whether we'd ever be on the receiving end of her slander.

Gossip has that kind of effect. It can give the perpetrator a bad reputation and breed mistrust between her and her audience. But how can we know whether we're gossiping or just sharing information?

Gossip gets a bad rap, but it wasn't always this way.

Research[50] shows that the word *gossip*, originally derived from "godparent," was used to describe the network of women who gathered to support a new mother. Through the centuries—and due to misogyny—*gossip* has taken on a negative connotation and is now mostly used to describe women who indulge in vicious talk.

Most of us enjoy talking about different social norms and we're curious about other people's lives. But that's not the same thing as sitting in a room and disparaging someone for fun. That's next level.

Many sociologists and anthropologists would argue that gossip is necessary to maintain a thriving civilization. It is natural to talk about the details of other people's lives because it's how we learn about cultural norms, understand community expectations, and get information about who's a threat and who's an ally.

If I'm new to your neighborhood and you tell me to be careful about locking my doors at night because the man down the street has Alzheimer's and has been known to wander, it teaches me about who to trust, what to be aware of, and what's happening in the environment around me.

The problem comes when the conversation about other people is *destructive*—infusing rumors, speculation, and a little bit of extra "flavor" to the story.

As linguist Deborah Tannen says, the question to ask yourself is whether the language you're using is "talking about" or "talking against."

For many women, the closer they are to a friend, the less "frowned upon" gossip becomes. The trust and history shared between two women helps to contextualize her character; we know she's not a bad person and we trust that we will be the exception to her gossip with others.

But, generally speaking, gossip is not only destructive to the subject being evaluated, but to the friendship of the women engaged in the activity. It can limit their potential for openness and vulnerability with each other. It can lead to feelings of guilt if they leave gossipy exchanges regretting their behavior. It can teach them to measure their words with each other to protect themselves from being the next "victim."

And when one friend is more comfortable with gossip than the other, both internal and external conflict will follow.

Having a gossipy friend can make you feel complicit and disloyal, but it can be difficult to know how to pull away without affecting the friendship overall. Here are a few ideas to consider about what might be going on behind the scenes.

Possibility 1. She's trying to bond with you.

Even though your friend's gossip is problematic, it may be well intentioned.

Research[51] shows that if two people share a negative attitude toward something, it *can* make them feel connected to each other (even more than sharing a positive attitude toward something!). That's because it feels like they've formed an alliance—they're in on something exclusive that the "outsider" (the subject of their dislike) can't access.

And when you consider how the interaction unfolds, it makes sense. When a friend shares a speculation about someone, we tend to weave our own commentary into the story, delight in the whispers, and prompt our friend for more information. In doing this dance, we become coconspirators, partnering in our mutual dislike and intrigue.

But the problem is that this strategy for manufacturing closeness isn't sustainable. It may initially bring us together, but since it also invites distrust between participants and threatens a capacity for vulnerability, it's not helpful in the effort to create (or sustain) an open and trusting friendship.

For the friend who often invites you to gossip, consider the possibility that it's less about her sinister behavior and more about her operating with what she's learned as a reliable strategy to connect with other women.

Possibility 2. She's insecure.

Putting excessive attention on other people's lives allows you to deflect from your own.

Your friend may also disparage another woman in the hopes that you'll see that person in a bad light, and, by extension, favor her more instead. This would position her closer to you than the other woman, making her feel more secure in where she stands with you.

Gossip is also a means of assessing our position within the social hierarchy of our network. The person sharing information has access, and she chooses who she will invite into the circle of knowledge.

And learning about how others are living, failing, coping, and succeeding helps us gauge how we are doing by comparison. For a woman who is not secure or who has low self-worth, this practice may be her attempt to (mentally) situate herself in a higher position. When she hears that someone had a tummy tuck, she feels better about her insecurities around her size because at least she didn't "cheat." When she learns about the recent scandal in someone's relationship, she feels less upset about being single. If she discovers that a new friend wears a wig, she may feel better about her own thinning hair. The woman who's obsessed with a friend's financial situation may be anxious about her own.

Research[52] suggests that, although both men and women gossip, men often do it to impress the receiver; women are more inclined to do it in attempt to damage the rival.

The truth is, these discoveries are often irrelevant to the lives of those gossiping, but they can offer a (false and fleeting) sense of security and relief for the one who is insecure.

Possibility 3. She's bored.

Gossip is titillating and appeals to our natural curiosity about others' lives. The content of women's conversation tends to lean toward the exploration[53] of social norms and the developments of other's lives.

For someone who doesn't have an active or fulfilling life, gossiping may be a pleasant escape from an otherwise humdrum day—welcome entertainment to fill her time. If her life is anticlimactic, gossip may have an especially intriguing appeal because it satisfies her desire to escape her own reality.

What to Do

If you have a friend whose habit of gossiping has begun to negatively shape the way you feel about her, try one or more of the following responses to shut it down.

Response 1. Model reform.

One way to discourage your friend from pulling you into her latest gossip fest is to let her know that you're trying to be more conscious of that habit yourself. Tell her that you are working on gossiping less, to signal that it's something you intentionally want to avoid.

This doesn't have to be awkward or judgmental—it's all in your delivery.

Try this:

"You know what? I'm trying to be better about gossiping, so even though I definitely have some things I want to add to this conversation—trust me!—I'm going to stay silent on this one."

This response allows you to commiserate with her, without calling it out and appearing self-righteous. This approach can also be effective if it inspires her to be more mindful of how often she's engaging in gossip as she works to follow your lead.

Response 2. Show your "but."

Let's say a group of friends begin to discuss a new friend's spending habits. You can stop their momentum by countering negative suppositions with positive ones.

Here's the formula: *"I don't know about [topic] but I do know that she [related positive trait about subject]."*

If they say, "Apparently Tiffany spent her entire rent check on clothes from that new boutique," you might respond with:

"I don't know anything about how she spends her money *but* I know that woman has incredible style, so I'm not surprised to hear that she likes to shop there."

This is a subtle way to signal that you're only interested in participating in the conversation if it's positive, otherwise, you don't plan to entertain the negative speculation. It also alters the direction of the conversation and may dissuade others from continuing (or at the very least, from expecting you to participate).

Response 3. Go silent, then redirect.

Gossip requires a captive audience to thrive, so if you want to put an end to things, you'll have to become a boring, inactive audience member.

Essentially, you'll have to become the absolute worst person to gossip with.

Try this: The next time your friend mentions someone's "walk of shame" or lack of personal style, just look away, give no response, and meet her comments with total silence. It might be awkward at first, but that's kind of the point.

After waiting a beat or two, change the subject. Break into something like, "Have you listened to [amazing musician]'s new album? I'm starting to feel like I'm the only person on the planet who hasn't heard it yet…" It's likely that she'll follow your lead and join you in the pivot. But if she asks why you didn't respond to what she said, offer something like, "Oh, well, I'm kind of over talking about her, I guess."

Demonstrating a lack of interest in gossip can be a passive yet effective way of discouraging it.

Response 4. Show empathy.

Let's say your friends are talking about someone who recently had to downsize her home. You might say something like, "I just feel bad. I know if people knew about my money struggles, I'd be mortified, so I almost don't even want to know about what she's got going on…"

Adopting and sharing the perspective of the subject not only gives them something new to consider, but it tends to stop the momentum for those who are delighting in the conversation. It's a nice way of saying, "I won't participate because I wouldn't want others doing this to me."

When to Let Go

If most of the time you spend together revolves around speculating about others' lives, you aren't investing much time and attention on the friendship itself—you've just built a habit of discussing other women—a practice that simply isn't fruitful (and possibly destructive). What else do you two have in common? Why do you continue to invest in the relationship?

You may also consider ending the friendship if you find that you're becoming increasingly suspicious or uneasy. Perhaps she's talking to you only to dig up dirt to share with others. Every time a friend shares information about someone else, she's signaling that she doesn't respect the "vault" she has with the subject of her gossip, one of the primary laws of the Secrecy Affinity.

You might also begin to dislike the way you feel about yourself. There's something about listening to gossip that makes us feel complicit, and if you leave the discussion feeling badly because it was clear your friend took pleasure in belittling someone else, the friendship might be toxic.

One objective of relationships is to feel known, which requires us to share ourselves. But when we're friends with someone who's demonstrating a lack of respect for others' privacy (humanity), you may determine that the friendship is no longer emotionally safe.

If you are content with being surface-level "activity buddies" without the expectation of platonic intimacy, you may be able to move forward with the friendship. But if gossip is a barrier to you feeling like your best self, you may want to dissolve the relationship.

How to Know Whether You're the "Gossip"

Sometimes it's hard to tell whether the conversations you're having about other people qualify as innocent storytelling or destructive speculation. Here are some signs that you may have fallen into the habit of gossiping about others:

Take stock of the recent conversations you've had with friends. Have you noticed that they don't share as much as they used to? Do they clam up when you start talking about others? Do they ever seem like they're defending the person you're talking about? These could be signs that others in your circle are uncomfortable with or disapprove of the conversation.

Another thing to consider is whether you're saying things about other women that you wouldn't say if those same women were present. And before you say, "I don't care, I'll say it to her face," think about whether saying it to her face would actually cause drama. If so, it could be an indicator that you're gossiping.

Finally, pay attention to the role you play in your friend group. Do they come to you first when they hear a new piece of gossip about someone? Do they make jokes about how you're always "in the know" about other people's business? Are you the person they ask for updates on other people's lives? These could all point to the fact that they view you as the resident reporter, and you'll have to decide if you're comfortable with that reputation.

Having a reputation for being a gossip may unintentionally isolate you from certain social circles if women know that you're someone with whom they have to keep their guard up. It can also be detrimental to your existing friendships if women in your life begin to feel that they must measure their words and actions when they're with you, for fear that you'll share the information with others.

There are many barriers to closeness and vulnerability in friendship, and gossip is a contributing factor that often flies under the radar, but if you take the time to steadily reduce how you engage, you may see more meaningful conversations happen with your friends.

The Love-Obsessed Friend

I was waist deep in a work project when she called.

"I'm so over it, Danni!" Amber often began her calls in the middle of an idea, so I was forced to play catch-up.

"What? What happened?"

She paused before revealing the reason behind her exasperation.

"It's Robert. He hasn't texted me back."

I sighed and dropped my shoulders, irritated but relieved that her issue wasn't more serious.

"Oh, okay. Well...when did you text him?"

"Ten minutes ago."

"Ten *minutes* ago?"

"Yeah..."

"I mean, is it possible he's on the toilet or something?"

"I know it sounds dumb, but I just never know what I'm gonna get with him and I'm over it."

What Amber didn't realize was that I was over it too. We were coworkers and became close pretty quickly. But when she got caught up in a new romance, I felt that she was oceans away.

The dating drama strained our friendship, but somehow we were still hanging on. Despite her habit of canceling plans with me when a guy would make a last-minute request to see her. Despite one-sided conversations where I endured monologues about her latest love interest while waiting for my turn to speak. Despite frequent changes to her personality, shapeshifting according to the preferences of her boyfriends.

One day, we were sipping wine while talking on the phone when she got the idea to break into an ex-boyfriend's house. I thought she was joking until

I heard keys jingle in the background. She was determined to know whether he had another girl over, and my desperate pleas did nothing to stop it.

She was in too deep. And so was I.

For much of our friendship, I felt like an underappreciated accomplice. As outspoken as I am, there was something about Amber that made me endure the dating drama. I appreciated virtually everything else about her: her humor, generosity, and creativity. But the more she poured into her romantic relationships, the less access I had to the very parts of her I loved so much.

I eventually grew exhausted of the friendship's unpredictability and lack of emotional reciprocity, but I struggled with my decision for years afterward. Did I give up on her too soon? Did I judge too harshly? If I were a more loyal friend would I have simply endured the chaos?

It can be difficult to stand by as a woman you love continually chooses to put a love interest above herself—and her friendships. How do you support her when the "advancement" of her dating life comes at the cost of her relationship with you?

How exactly are we to manage conflict with our "love-obsessed" friends?

Know the Signs

Look at the following list to know whether you're dealing with a love-obsessed friend. She:

- Seems desperate in the way she talks about love
- Cancels plans with you to spend time with her new crush
- Dominates your conversation with her dating drama
- Often needs you to "rescue" her from some romantic crisis
- Seems uneasy when she's apart from her partner
- Disappears whenever she gets a partner
- Sometimes denies or excuses her love interest's bad behavior

If you've ever had a love-obsessed friend, you know what it's like to be at the mercy of her whims. One day, she's swearing off men for the last time; the next day, she's ditching you to spend time with someone she met at the grocery store who might be "the one." Like any good friend, you support her at each turn because you want her to be happy. But there may come a point when you want to get off the roller coaster that is her chaotic dating life.

What makes these friendships so delicate is the internal conflict between wanting to encourage her journey of finding "the one" and holding an intense aversion to the entire process.

When dealing with a love-obsessed friend, you may begin to feel like your only purpose is to help her through her latest romantic dilemma, and it can be exhausting.

Getting Perspective

Let's examine a few possible reasons for your friend's behavior:

Possibility 1. She's under pressure from the patriarchy.

When generations of women have been raised on movies that tell them the story's not over until the girl's got her guy, it's not surprising that they'd apply that framework to their real lives.

Your friend's "obsession" may be rooted in a deeply ingrained message about a woman's value and fulfillment resting in her being "partnered."

And who can blame her when that message is reinforced nearly everywhere she turns, including:

- A slew of cultural rituals to celebrate romantic partnership
- Family members who constantly ask whether she's "seeing anyone special"
- Friends who get married one by one, assuring her that she'll eventually find "the one" when it's time

- Older women who are eyed with suspicion as people wonder how it's possible for them to have never "found someone"

Despite an increasing number of singles and new narratives about what it means to design a life without romantic partnership, the perception of single women as unfulfilled and lonely lives on. And if everyone assumes that your friend will be unhappy until she finds someone to claim her— well, she just might start to believe it.

So, is it any wonder why some women would devote so much time and energy to finding their "person," even to the detriment of their friendships?

For the woman who's bought in and doubled down, her friends get a front-row seat to her focused pursuit of partnership. They may feel neglected as they're reduced to sounding boards and placeholders. They wait patiently as every conversation somehow turns back to her latest love interest. They forgive over and over when she cancels plans at the last minute to cater to his whims. They fight to make her see her worth, only to have her put yet another man above the friendship—above herself.

But when those friends are up against a force as powerful as patriarchal expectations, it's hard to compete.

Possibility 2. She might be a love addict. (No, seriously.)

I'll admit, when I first learned about sex and love addiction, I rolled my eyes.

I thought, *"Boy crazy," maybe. A "romantic," perhaps. But an* addict?

So, I spoke with Kerry Cohen, author of *Crazy for You*[54] and a psychotherapist who specializes in women's sex and love addiction.

She helped me understand that love addiction, while categorized by professionals as a diagnosis, is really just a symptom of other things like cultural pressures and attachment issues. It manifests in women as "obsessive craving and intrusive thinking"[55] as they seek their next dopamine surge, oftentimes at the expense of their own well-being.

And naturally, this impacts their friendships.

Per Kerry, "The main thing about being a love addict and having female friendships is that it's misunderstood. People don't always know about it. So, it looks like your friend is [just] making the same stupid choices again and again and won't change her behavior."

I felt a ping of guilt as Kerry explained people's lack of tolerance. I began immediately thinking of times friends repeatedly returned to awful men. While outwardly I empathized, I was seething on the inside. I didn't understand why they couldn't be stronger, how they could subject themselves to someone who didn't recognize how wonderful they were. I judged swiftly and often, confused as to why they'd choose to bend for a man who paid them no mind while her friends waited patiently on the sidelines, ready to give her the love she was due.

"When you're a feminist and all your friends are feminists, it's hard. Sex and love addicts are typically professionals with lots of success in their personal lives. But it's like, here they are spending all day thinking of some 'dumb boy'? But friends can have compassion [for their friend] in the same way they would for any other issue."

Consider the possibilities that your friend's "love obsession" may be caused by a matrix of factors, including her background, propensity for dependency, trauma, and genetics. While it may still negatively impact your friendship, it helps to depersonalize her behavior and extend more grace to the cycle she might find herself in.

Possibility 3: She may be in an abusive relationship.

If you notice that your friend starts behaving differently in a relationship, consider the possibility that her partner may be mistreating her. We often assume this kind of mistreatment will present itself in obvious ways—waiting to see our friend walking around with a black eye—but the signs might be a bit more subtle.

If she is withdrawing from friends, beginning to dress differently, anxious when she misses her partner's calls, or on the receiving end of their insults and bad behavior, she may be in an unhealthy—even abusive—relationship.

When you address it, approach her with gentleness and try opening your conversation with something like, "Hey, I've noticed [list of tangible changes], and I'm worried about you." Remember that she may feel a certain loyalty to and responsibility for her partner, so try not to blame them or you'll risk her pushing you away. They may also want to isolate her from people who don't support their relationship so tread lightly.

It might be frustrating to see her return to an abusive partner, but try to remain nonjudgmental. She'll be more likely to leave the relationship if she feels confident that she has supportive friends to turn to. You can also prepare resources so that when she is open to hearing you out, you'll be ready.

What to Do

Once you've gained a bit of perspective and compassion for your friend's situation, you might be ready to take action on the issue.

Response 1. Be honest about how it's impacting you.

You may continue to accommodate your friend's behavior or suppress your frustration but you can only do that for so long. Eventually, you'll either end up exploding on her or become passive-aggressive to subtly signal your displeasure.

Speaking directly may be the most effective way to communicate your concerns and make her aware of what's on your mind.

I encourage you to be transparent, even though it may be a sensitive subject for her. It's okay to tell her that she hurt your feelings. Talking honestly is important, but remember not to judge, because we are all flawed.

Avoid guilting her or making her choose. Instead, stick to the facts. Try this:

"I feel [feeling] whenever [factual, observable action] happens. Help me out."

Example: "I feel confused about how to offer support when your feelings about Brian change from day to day. Help me out."

Responding this way places the focus on how you feel and requires her to collaborate with you to find a solution. It's a way to humbly ask for her behavior to change without being accusatory.

Response 2. Avoid giving her an ultimatum.

You may be so desperate to extract yourself from her odyssey of love that you try to force her into one clear, definitive direction. But presenting options as an "either/or" can backfire.

The thing about ultimatums is that you must be emotionally prepared for an outcome you don't like. Friendships must allow each person some sense of autonomy, giving a friend the right to her own choices and perspectives. It's important that people don't lose the right to govern themselves when they enter a relationship, but ultimatums remove their right to choose for themselves, and may create feelings of indignation and resentment.

To be clear: Setting a boundary with a friend is different from giving her an ultimatum, in that a boundary focuses on communicating limitations, not controlling her behavior. Show her that you respect her right to choose by allowing her the space to work through her romantic relationships according to her own timeline.

Response 3. Stop perpetuating the idea that she needs to find someone.

While your friend's love fixation may sometimes frustrate you, consider the ways in which you may unknowingly contribute to the issue.

You may also add pressure to the pursuit when you ask about when she'll "settle down" or when you tell her that she'll find "the one." You mean well (and it might be true!), but your attempts to reassure her are also perpetuating the idea of a "finish line"—one that she is working desperately to reach.

Be aware of the times when you speak of singleness as an affliction and partnership as a remedy. These ideas have the potential to fuel the impulses of friends who are already laser-focused on their romantic endeavors.

When to Let Go

If you've decided it's time to end your friendship, make sure your decision isn't rooted in judgment of her character. Let's be honest: if we ended relationships with other women because we disagreed with their romantic choices, we'd all be friendless.

The real issue here is one of purpose and endurance. Once you begin to question these two things, you'll have clarity on whether it's time to leave.

If the primary function of your role in the friendship is to act as a placeholder or a prop, you'll eventually grow tired of not getting the same love, support, and attention that you're providing.

And if you have been physically, mentally, and emotionally drained by the upkeep required to maintain the friendship, you may have to let go for the sake of self-preservation.

Do you feel that your friend really sees you? Does she extend the same amount of curiosity and intention about your life as you do for her? If so, then while she may be quite focused on her love life, it sounds like she's still found a way to prioritize you as well. But when you begin to notice that your friend only uses you as a temporary distraction from the ongoing saga that is her dating life, you'll become resentful in your fight to receive the same care and attention.

You should also be on alert if this friendship has had negative ripple effects in other areas of your life. If...

- her last-minute cancellations impact the time you're able to spend with others
- your complaints about the friendship have begun to dominate your conversation with others

- you feel sad or irritable after spending time with your friend and that mood carries over into other relationships

You may decide it's not worth it to stay in a situation that affects how you show up in other areas of your life.

Letting go of a love-obsessed friend can stir a lot of inner turmoil because you may feel that you're betraying the unwritten girl code to ride or die for a friend through her ups and downs. How many movies have we seen of the friend who endures her friend's crazy antics, dissecting every text, joining her for midnight drive-bys, listening to every new dramatic development...? In the real world, there are limits.

This does not make you disloyal. This does not make you a fair-weather friend.

This makes you a woman who loves herself enough to preserve her sanity while loving her friend from a distance.

How to Know Whether You're the Love-Obsessed Friend

Sometimes in our pursuit to feel loved, we can lose our grip on the friendships that have kept us steady. We underestimate their resilience, testing their capacity each time we choose to neglect them in the face of an opportunity for romance.

If you believe that your friendships don't need the same attention as a romantic partner, you may end up putting them on the back burner. If you feel entitled to friends' unwavering time, attention, and energy to carry you through your ongoing romantic crises just because they're your friends, you may be unintentionally taking advantage of their love for you.

Consider the ways in which your choices for your partner have negative consequences in your friendships. Are friends often left wondering when you'll show up (physically or emotionally)?

Does your relationship drama dominate conversations with other women? Do you often make promises to your friends about how you will operate in your relationships, only to break them later? When you weigh the energy you give to your love interest against what you give to your friends, is there balance? Would any of your friends be able to say they feel neglected when you're involved in a romantic partnership?

While you value your friends, you may risk losing them if their experience of the friendship is not one where they *feel* valued.

This can be reconciled by doing a check-in. The next time you're with a friend, say this:

"How are we doing? What's one thing I could do to be a better friend to you?"

Even though it's your friend's responsibility to communicate any dissatisfaction, you can get proactive about ensuring that your friends feel seen and heard in your relationship. Use her feedback to help you determine what changes need to be made, if any, to keep the friendship strong.

Then, affirm her, letting her know how much she means to you. This can do wonders for reassuring her when she begins to question her significance in your life. Be honest about your desires, weaknesses, and intentions to recalibrate and bring you both back to a place of understanding and connection.

The Controlling Friend

You should've seen this coming.

After casually mentioning to Samantha—your coworker turned bestie—that you were struggling to complete this year's annual report, you suddenly find yourself sitting in your office with her barking "suggestions for improvement" in your ear.

Samantha's pushiness has been beneficial for her career advancement, but being on the receiving end as a friend can be overbearing. If she's not telling you what to do at work, she's making decisions about where you two go to happy hour and telling you how to respond to texts from your crush and planning every detail of every girls' trip.

And you're beginning to feel trapped.

You're a relatively mellow person, so you've spent the past three years going with the flow. But lately, you've been wondering why you continue to let Samantha take the reins. You love her sense of humor and the way that she has your back whenever you need support, but how do you reconcile those positive traits with her incessant need for control?

What do you do when her demands leave little room for your feelings and preferences?

How do you maintain a friendship with a woman who's only satisfied when things go her way?

Know the Signs

Here are a few signs that you're dealing with a controlling friend:

- She takes personal offense if you choose differently.

- She may use tactics like guilting or manipulation to get you to do what she wants.
- She believes that if things don't go her way, everything will fall apart.
- She's unable to see various paths to the same outcome.
- She becomes irritable over seemingly small things.
- She doesn't manage emotions well when things don't go her way.
- You can't remember the last time she admitted she was wrong.

Getting Perspective

The average person is not devastated or immobilized by things not going their way. They're able to adapt, accept reality, and move forward. But those with controlling tendencies have a proclivity to use various tactics to manage the outcome of every situation.

If you're doing something your friend doesn't like, she may use passive-aggression to show her disapproval, in hopes that you'll stop the behavior. If you want to go to a certain restaurant but it's not the one that she suggested, she may act irrationally or pout to make you feel guilty about your choice so that you'll eventually give in.

The reason this trait threatens healthy friendships is that it doesn't leave room for each person to show up as their full self. If a friend must share the same opinions or bend to someone else's will in order to keep the peace, it is not a relationship among two equals. Trying to create certain outcomes by influencing a friend's behavior is controlling, and it suffocates others' sense of agency—a critical component of any mature and healthy friendship.

But it's possible your friend doesn't know she's doing it, let alone that it's affecting your relationship, so it's worth taking the time to understand why she operates this way.

Possibility 1. She's operating from a place of fear or distrust.

If it's difficult for your friend to trust that others can competently and effectively manage a situation, she may try to control them in an effort to make sure things go according to the (very specific) ideas that she has in mind. Controlling people spend their time trying to make the outside world match their internal vision of the way things should be, and they rarely trust others to be able to make that vision a reality.

She may also be terrified that things will fall apart if she's not the one handling the reins. If your friend is trying to protect herself from what she anticipates as an unfavorable outcome, she may feel more secure controlling the situation.

Possibility 2. She doesn't have control in other areas of her life.

Take a look at the parts of her life where she doesn't have a voice. It's important for people to have a sense of agency, but if this has been taken away from her at work, in her family dynamics, or in areas like her health or finances, she may be working to reclaim that sense of control by overcompensating in her friendships.

Possibility 3. Your girl may have anxiety.

A need for control is one of the primary signs of anxiety. Other signs may include irritability, constant worrying and fretfulness, difficulty sleeping, and restlessness. If your friend has an anxiety disorder (which nearly 1 in 4 women do),[56] she may be controlling in her relationships in an effort to feel at peace.

If you feel like she's controlling, it might be less about wanting you to be her robot, and more about her trying to ensure certain outcomes to make her feel less anxious and helpless.

What to Do

Response 1. Appeal to her sensibilities.

With a controlling personality, it's easy to become hyperfocused on the outcome of a situation, getting caught up in the details. This makes it hard to take an aerial view to keep things in perspective. If you're in a situation where your friend is set on having you do things a certain way, try posing a question that helps her realize what really matters.

Try this:

"I know that restaurant really appeals to you, but the rest of the group wants to eat at the place downtown. At the end of the day, all that matters is we eat some good food and have a good time together, right?"

She'll either acquiesce or try to justify her position—either way, you've made it clear that you have the same goal—there just may be different ways of achieving it.

Response 2. Ask about her fears.

It's possible that your friend is holding tightly to her ideas of how things should be because she's fearful of what would happen if she didn't. If she's adamant about how you two spend the upcoming weekend, it might be driven less by her desire for a particular set of plans and more by her fears of what would happen if you don't do things her way. If she's irritated because you're not getting as excited as she is about something, explore what she may be afraid of.

Try this:

"It seems like you have a really particular vision for this. What do you fear will happen if things don't go the way you want?"

This approach shows genuine concern while also getting at the heart of the matter. It may also be the kind of response that comes in handy when what you really want to say is "Girl, I'm gonna need you to stop acting like a control freak," which . . . probably wouldn't help.

Response 3. Inform her of the impact.

Depending on the severity of your friend's controlling nature, you may have to directly state the impact it has on your friendship. Help her to see the connection between her need to be right and the tension that it causes.

Try this:

"I'm not sure if you realize it, but sometimes when I voice a different opinion than you, the mood shifts. You withdraw/give the silent treatment/yell at me [or some other factual, observable behavior], and it makes me think that if I want to keep the peace in our friendship, I have to agree with you. Am I off base here?"

You can even go one step further by showing her the dilemma she puts you in each time she tries to control what you say or do:

"I'm torn because I want you to be happy, but I also want to have a say in [situation]. I'm struggling because I don't think I should have to choose between the two."

Helping your friend to see that her behavior has a very real impact on the friendship may encourage her to rethink her approach. If she values your friendship, she should trust your feedback and be willing to humble herself long enough to see things from your perspective.

When to Let Go

If you confront your friend but she lacks self-awareness, she may struggle to see your feedback as valid, which means your efforts to make her stop controlling you may be in vain.

It's one thing if your friend has a type A personality and is serious about controlling little details in her own life. But if her need to control extends to her relationships, then the people around her will inevitably begin to distance themselves.

If your friend is employing manipulative tactics like guilting you, giving disapproving looks, or becoming passive aggressive (meaning she's not going to explicitly state what she wants but she'll certainly find other ways to make it known), she doesn't respect your having your own mind. While she may be a good friend in other aspects—generous, funny, and supportive—it's likely that you only have access to these traits to the degree that you're willing to accommodate her.

You should never feel as if you're walking on eggshells or that you need to suppress your own desires to keep your friend happy and avoid confrontation. If you're beginning to feel inferior and find yourself second-guessing your decisions when you're together, it may be time to release your friend, because a healthy friendship allows (and encourages!) both parties to freely express themselves.

If you frequently have to give in to remain in good standing, she's not your friend; she's your boss.

And it may be time for you to resign.

How to Know Whether You're the Controlling Friend

Do you become irritated, nervous, or offended when your friends choose a path that's different from the one you'd like them to take? Do you feel personally slighted if you give advice and your friend chooses not to follow it? Do you change the way you engage with your friends (withdrawing, showing contempt) if they don't do what you've asked them to do?

If your friends make jokes about you being "the bossy one" or being "type A," then begin to pay attention to their reactions immediately following a difference of opinion. Do they seem frustrated or defeated when you explain your side? If they express themselves and you disagree, do you feel the need to launch a campaign to help them see that they're "wrong"?

Think about the areas in your life that you need full control over. Then, consider—honestly—whether your friendships are one of them. Being insistent about the things friends do or say can make them feel that you don't like them for who they are, only for how well they listen to you.

Remember that healthy friendships allow each person to have different opinions, goals, and standards. That shouldn't threaten you; it should excite you.

Remind yourself that when your friends choose differently than you, it's rarely personal. And then find ways to appreciate the things that make them truly unique, without needing to change, persuade, or control them.

The Jealous Friend

Your server walks away from the table, adding a few final scribbles to his pad to complete everyone's order. As he disappears into the throng of people bustling inside, you scan the faces of your three friends seated at the table.

Now is the perfect time.

"So, something big happened..." you say, mysteriously. You hate to admit you're drinking in this moment of anticipation, as their eyes dart over to you curiously.

"Wait—what? Girl, what did you do?" The most dramatic of the bunch wears an excited smile and begs you to fill them in.

"I...I applied for that promotion a few weeks ago that I was telling you about. And...I got it!"

The ladies explode into applause and raise their glasses to your announcement, and while you're beaming under the glow of their excitement, you can't help but notice that Jessica averts her eyes and sips her wine in silence.

"Y'all, I feel like a 'big girl.' I get an office, a company card, *and* I get to travel to really beautiful cities—all paid for. Insane, right?"

Everyone chatters excitedly, hyping you up for being the boss that you are. And that's when you notice Jessica whisper something to one of the ladies and roll her eyes.

It's the third time she's done something that made you suspect that she may be...jealous.

But how do you address something like that?

How can you tell if your friend really *is* hating on you or if it's all just in your head?

Know the Signs

Here are a few telltale signs of envy:

- Sarcastic comments in response to your good news
- Withdrawing or changing the subject when you are in the spotlight
- Regularly pointing out flaws or inadequacies
- Lack of support for your endeavors or achievements
- Attempts to sabotage your opportunities
- Diminishing your accomplishments

One of these signs in isolation may not mean much at all, but if a combination of these behaviors happen pretty regularly, it might be worth looking at.

Getting Perspective

Before we jump in, it's important to know the difference between jealousy and envy.

Most times, when people are talking about a "jealous" friend, what they are really describing is envy. Let me explain:

Envy involves two people. Jealousy requires three.

When you're envious, it means you want what someone else has (the issues is between two people). But when you're jealous of someone or something, it means you fear that what you have will be taken by a third party (the issue concerns three people).

An example of envy: Perhaps your friend just moved into a gorgeous new loft, and now you can't stop thinking about how *you* deserve a gorgeous loft too. It can be a relatively harmless feeling, if you channel it into a means of motivation. Seeing her achieve this goal may inspire you to take steps to be more intentional about building your savings. That's productive.

But if you begin to wonder why she got it because you deserve to have it instead (or worse: you begin plotting ways to take it for yourself!)—yeah, that would be problematic.

An example of jealousy: If your best friend begins spending a lot of time with a new woman she met at work and she can't stop talking about her, you might get nervous that you might slowly "lose" your friend to her new work bestie (oh, c'mon, we've all been there!).

So, as we discuss this topic, I'll be using the word *envy* to refer to the feelings you suspect your friend might be having when it comes to your success and achievements.

Now, when you begin to wonder whether your friend is envious of you, things can get awkward. You don't want to seem like you're full of yourself, and you certainly don't want to entertain the idea that the friendship itself may not be as genuine as you'd believed. But how do you know whether a friend really *is* envious of you? And how do you address it without her thinking you're being conceited?

Whenever we discuss envy in friendship, we typically vilify the friend who's exhibiting those traits, but envy is sometimes a natural, knee-jerk response to situations that make us feel inadequate or insecure. It's not necessarily immediately indicative of disloyalty or ill will.

Once you accept that these moments are a natural part of the range of human emotions, it may help you to depersonalize the experience when it happens to you. Yes, there are times when consistent displays of envy are going to be hard to reconcile (especially if she's showing intent to harm, detract from, or sabotage). But, other times, it may be completely innocuous.

If you have a friend who has undoubtedly been showing signs of envy and you don't understand where it's coming from (or what it might mean for your friendship), consider a few things that might be influencing the dynamic from behind the scenes:

Possibility 1. She's navigating life with a fixed mind-set.

These days, you can't throw a rock without hitting a life coach who's in the middle of preaching about a "growth" mind-set. But the idea is popular for a reason, and it could be the root of your friend's feelings of envy.

Those with a "fixed" mind-set believe there to be limited opportunities available to them. But those with a growth mind-set view the world through a lens of abundance, seeing opportunity everywhere. Someone with this way of thinking can't help but to be threatened by another person's achievements, because they interpret it as meaning that there's less available for themselves.

A person with a fixed mind-set might also think their knowledge, abilities, and relationships are static, and there's no way to change or improve. But someone with a growth mind-set believes these things can be developed over time.

Let's say you're giving some of your girls a tour of your brand-new apartment. You notice that one of your friends has only commented on the chipped paint in the corner, the "tiny" closets, and horrible parking situation.

While the comments are certainly insensitive, you'll likely be tempted to draw conclusions that personalize her remarks:

Wow, is she really hating on my apartment right now?
Does she not want to see me happy?
Is she really my friend if she's going to say things like that?
I can't believe she doesn't support me . . .

But if she's living at home with her parents or if she's been dreaming of a better space for herself, your new lease may represent something bigger. She may see your *having* as her *lacking*. Her negative remarks aren't necessarily indicative of a desire to bring you down; they may reveal a general fixed mind-set. The fixed mind-set perceives someone else's access to the things that she desires for herself as a threat to her dreams of realizing the same achievement.

Possibility 2. Your past experiences with envy may have made you hypersensitive.

This issue came up in a coaching session when a client told me about getting phased out of a new friend group.

"Honestly, I think they're jealous of me. This happens *all the time*. I think it's because I'm more of an intellectual, and they're just not. Maybe they're jealous that they can't keep up with the kinds of conversations I like to have..."

She told me that she'd been picked on when she was younger for being a "nerd," and as an adult, her "bullying" didn't take the form of schoolyard teasing, but was now met with subtle exclusion and backhanded comments.

So, when her friends began to slowly stop inviting her, she immediately pointed to their being envious.

If you grew up with a mother who dismissed your conflict with a friend as "She's just jealous" (we often say "jealous" instead of "envious"), you may have built an association that followed through adulthood. If you find that your friends are often envious of you (and this is the narrative for *every* female friendship you've ever had), then something larger is at play here.

If you *often* suspect envy in your friendships, ask yourself the following questions to get some clarity around your friendship history:

a. How do *you* define envy? Is it a lack of praise or enthusiasm from a friend? Is it criticism? Think about the way you interpret certain behaviors as "hating" and reflect on how these interpretations might be leading to the same narrative.

b. Which "friendship pools" are you pulling from? Women who often exhibit envious, sabotaging, and resentful behaviors may struggle with their confidence and self-esteem. But women who are self-assured are able to find joy in others' success, unbothered. So, if having "jealous" friends is a common theme in your friendship history, it's worth asking:

Where do I make most of my friends? Is there a theme among the background, interests, or experiences with the people I welcome into my life? See whether you notice any patterns in your selection process that reveal any skewed motivations for befriending certain kinds of people.

c. How does your anticipation of being rejected affect the way you engage with your friends? Is it possible that the assumptions and beliefs you're carrying *into* these friendships is powering a self-fulfilling prophecy? Is it possible that if you are anticipating rejection from other women, you may be unknowingly exhibiting behavior that keeps them at an arm's length, creating the very distance you'll later perceive negatively?

If envy really is showing up in your friendships and you're noticing your friends are being sarcastic, withholding praise, or generally showing a lack of support around your achievements, there are a few actions you can take in an attempt to gain understanding and course correct (before deciding whether it's time to let the friendship go).

What to Do

The goal of highlighting reasons for your friend's envious behavior is to help you refrain from adopting a "me vs. her" mind-set and instead, to find a way to have compassion for where she's coming from.

But let's be real: your compassion doesn't make her habits any less annoying.

If you're convinced that your friend has exhibited envious behavior on more than one occasion, you may be ready to address it (or, for some of us, put your blinders on and act like it isn't happening). Remember, healthy conflict is all about finding understanding, so you can get on the same page and reconcile as quickly as possible, before things fester.

Here are four ways to take action:

Response 1. Call it out with a spirit of curiosity, not accusation.

One mistake we often make when we suspect a friend is jealous or envious is taking action based on our assumptions. But operating under a self-constructed narrative can have negative consequences.

Instead, try approaching the issue from a place of genuine curiosity.

If she made a sarcastic remark at brunch, *get curious* about what the remark meant.

If she didn't show up to your baby shower, *get curious* about whether things are okay on her end.

If she was the only one who didn't say you looked nice in your new dress, *get curious* about whether she was distracted by thoughts of her own, unrelated to what you were wearing.

The filter that you run these behaviors through can greatly alter the outcome of the friendship overall. Here's an exercise:

Complete the following chart to track the different friendship outcomes over time:

Think of a recent remark or behavior that you interpreted as envy:

> Assuming her remark was from a place of envy or resentment will likely make me feel [emotion], and because of that, I would probably react by [behavior]—which would likely result in [consequence/impact on the friendship].
>
> Accepting her remark as something coming from a place of personal distraction, insecurity, or genuine concern for me, I will likely feel [emotion]. From these feelings, I'd probably react by [behavior], and this could affect our overall friendship with that [consequence/impact].

Taking the time to get curious about her motives instead of assuming the worst can be a bridge or a breaking.

If you're ready to address it, remember to address the **factual observation** about what happened and pair it with a question for clarification or understanding.

The formula: [factual observation + question]

Here's how it looks in action:

Script 1: Hey, I noticed that the last few times I mentioned my new apartment, you seemed to withdraw a bit [factual observation]. Is everything okay [question for understanding]?

or

Script 2: When we were at brunch yesterday and I mentioned that Brian finally asked me out, you said something and I didn't know what to make of it [factual observation]. What did you mean when you said XYZ [questions for understanding]?

This approach is helpful because it gives your friend an opportunity to provide clarity. But don't assume you know how she'd respond until you try. She may confirm your suspicions in a moment of vulnerability ("Well, yeah, I guess I feel some kind of way because I thought *I'd* have an apartment by now . . ."); she may be oblivious to the impact of her behavior ("Oh my gosh, no, I didn't mean it like that. I'm sorry if it came off that way!"); she may deny the behavior ("Wait, what are you talking about? No, I didn't.")

If after these attempts you notice *the behavior continues*, your responses can get increasingly more direct. Try:

Script 3: You know you're one of my favorite people to celebrate good news with, right? But lately, I feel this distance/tension when I mention [subject]. I'm struggling because I want to be able to bring this stuff to you, but I don't like how I feel afterward.

Either way, your goal should be to explore your friend's perspective in an ongoing effort to create understanding between you two. Your first instinct should not be to interpret her actions as being against you, but if the goal is to create harmony, you must understand that your first line of defense is against division itself. This is best achieved by confronting a friend with a spirit of curiosity over accusation.

Response 2. Show appreciation for the ways she does show up.

This response may seem counterintuitive, because if you suspect a friend is envious of you in any way, you may want to respond with distance and/or defensiveness. But the goal is to reconcile (or at least get clarity) as quickly as possible, remember?

Instead, to remind her that you two are on the same team, find a way to acknowledge the ways she does show up for you.

She criticized your new apartment? After the tour, thank her for taking the time to drive up and share this moment with you because it wouldn't be the same without her.

She said that the only reason you aced that exam is because you got lucky? Thank her for being such a good study buddy and let her know how nice it is to have finally found a friend who supports your studies.

She changed the subject when you share that your new boyfriend took you on the most romantic date of your life? Tell her how much you appreciate her listening when you were processing your feelings about him, because her attentiveness contributed to the happiness you feel today.

But, Danielle, am I supposed to act like I didn't notice?

This is not a matter of denial or pretending. It's about choosing what you give attention to. People tend to repeat the behavior that gets rewarded, so you're not only reminding your friend that you two are on the same team (which might help ease any anxiety or dissatisfaction she may feel), but you're also subconsciously encouraging her to exhibit more of the positive behavior she does display.

Response 3. Continue being proud of your achievements.

One common mistake we make when we sense a friend may be envious is to downplay our excitement or to abandon the subject entirely. But no one should have to minimize their joy to make others comfortable. Whether you're a mom who's proud of her kid's blossoming reading skills or a college graduate who just landed her dream job, your friends should be there ready to join in your excitement. Life can be so difficult and messy and unpredictable, so when we have these moments worth celebrating, we want to make the most of them.

Sure, if your friend is in a financial crisis, it might not be sensitive to mention the back-to-back bonuses you received at work every time you two get together. But to mention it once and have her congratulate you is totally fine—it's what friends do. We delight in each other's joy.

As long as you're mindful of your own motivations when celebrating certain achievements, you should feel free to celebrate them with the friends you love (and who love you).

Response 4: Don't call her "jealous."

Asking, "Are you jealous or something?" has literally never helped.

Literally. Never. Helped. Don't do it. You've been warned.

When to Let Go

One of the great benefits of friendship is to be fully known and accepted. But if you begin to feel that you must withhold or downplay your highs for another person's comfort, you'll never be able to reap the full benefits of healthy and supportive female friendships.

If *after* you've exercised all the response options, you're *still* experiencing the signs of envy listed above, you may need to distance yourself from that friendship.

Let me be clear: This does not mean that she should be instantly vilified. When people inevitably ask why your friendship ended, you'll be tempted to write her off as "the jealous friend" who couldn't be happy for you, saying things like "I just had to, like, let that toxic energy out of my life."

Instead, leave from a place of compassion for both her and yourself. It may be possible that she is in a life season that makes it hard for her to show up for others authentically right now. She may be struggling with certain insecurities or habits that inevitably impact her ability to be a good friend to others. And while she works through that, you have chosen not to be partnered in that friendship, because it would ultimately negatively impact *your* needs.

You should be able to show up without measuring every word or being on guard with suspicions that your friend might be trying to actively diminish your achievements. There's no emotional safety to bring your full self to the table.

In a healthy friendship, you should be able to celebrate your "wins" alongside women who want nothing but the best for you. Because these women don't feel that they're in competition with us. They share in your success because you're so close that it feels like their own.

How to Know Whether You're the "Jealous" Friend

The problem with having a conversation about envy is that no one wants to claim it. It's such a deeply unappealing quality that the idea of being plagued by it is reprehensible.

But it can't be that everyone else is the problem. The truth: sometimes, it's *us*.

We've all been in a space where—because of what we perceived as a lack in our own life—we've found it difficult to be 100 percent happy for someone else's moment.

The trick is to check yourself immediately when it happens, and work to hold tightly to this truth: your friend's beauty, professional accomplishments, relationship status, and charisma have literally nothing to do with your personal trajectory, resources, or opportunities.

What God has for her, is for her; what God has for you, is for you.

There is no benefit to comparing.

If it's envy that you're struggling with (wishing you had what your friend has), it can be helpful if you zoom out for a moment. Remember that you and your friend are peers; try to stop viewing her as someone who's "ahead" whenever she accomplishes something. It might also help to think of all the ways you two are similar to help you see how within reach those achievements are for you as well.

For example, when my first kid was only a few months old, I was sleep-deprived and starting to get cabin fever from being cooped up in the house with a fussy baby. So, when a friend of mine came to visit and began telling me about her upcoming trip to Las Vegas (something I couldn't afford at that time), I felt a little envious.

I gave her a sarcastic "Hmph, well, that must be nice..." and instantly regretted it. My friend grew silent and walked to the other side of the room, unsure of how to respond.

"Hey," I tried to recover quickly. "Sorry. I'm being petty. I guess I'm just so tired of being in the house with the baby all day and could just use a little break. But I'm so glad you're finally going—it's been on your bucket list for a while. How long are you staying?"

If you're in a season that makes it particularly hard to show up enthusiastically for a friend, you might:

- Make snarky comments after a friend just shared a win
- Secretly wonder how your friend earned/deserves that promotion/ relationship
- Try to figure out what she has that you don't
- Get quiet after she mentions getting something that you've been wanting for yourself

Take some time to yourself to explore why certain subjects give you such a strong response, and do the inner work to get to a place where you can be happy for others. If you don't, it will directly impact your ability to show up as a friend.

The Newly Changed Friend

While video-chatting with your friend Ava, you begin to notice that she seems distracted. You're in the middle of talking about an upcoming music show when she loses interest, which is wild when you remember how excited she used to get about any opportunity to see her favorite bands live. But tonight, she seems bored by the whole conversation.

"Apparently, it's gonna be a really great lineup," you say in an effort to stir a bit of enthusiasm. But she remains unfazed.

You decide to change the subject to recapture her attention.

"So, how are you and Marcus? Is he still pretending he doesn't know how to clean so that you'll have to do it?" You laugh, expecting that she will too.

"I really wish you wouldn't talk down about him like that. He's actually been a lot better about it, y'know?"

"Oh, I'm sorry. I wasn't trying to be rude…" You're confused. Making jokes about Marcus's helplessness used to be a staple of your conversations, but apparently now it offends her?

"I've really had my head down studying to get this license so I can finally get into real estate…." Ava became interested in real estate two years ago after binge-watching some show about luxury houses, and you didn't realize she was going to pursue it seriously. Hadn't she wanted to pursue her fashion career just a few months earlier?

"…I've been studying with Tanya and a few of her friends. It's been really helpful."

You've never been the jealous type, so you don't mind that Ava has other friends. But doesn't Tanya's crew subscribe to a few ideologies that you know to be highly problematic? Would Ava soon be talking and thinking like them?

So much has changed lately. You and Ava used to be more playful; she used to be a free spirit who wasn't obsessed with finance podcasts and soy milk (or underperforming boyfriends, yet here we are). It's become really difficult to look at her without thinking, *"Who* are *you?"*

Whenever you hint at the ways she's changed, she seems irritated, so you've decided not to push. But it's been difficult to relate to her in this new season of her life, and it's hard to know whether you two will end up drifting apart because of it.

Getting Perspective

When clients talk to me about a friend who's changed, they usually begin by rattling off a list of all her new habits. It's clear they're feeling frustrated with—and even betrayed by—their friend's new life.

The first thing we must do to stay in harmony is realize that the source of the conflict is not our friend—it's *change* itself.

When a woman you love begins to go down an unfamiliar path, you have to remember that if you're friends for long enough, you *will* witness a change at some point. The challenge becomes figuring out ways to maintain (and even strengthen) your friendship when the landscape ahead looks completely foreign.

Whether she's become a mother, a vegan, or an advocate for political issues we don't support, our friend's changing worldviews can elicit several different emotions...

We may feel angry because she's violated an unspoken agreement that our friendship remain rooted in the values and dynamics we shared when we first came together. We may feel insecure because a shift in hobbies or priorities forces us to question the role we now play in her life—how big, how small, how significant.

We may feel abandoned or excluded, watching from the sidelines as she immerses herself in a new world (oftentimes with new people speaking a new language). We may feel helpless, having no control (and little influence) as she drifts away from what we know.

Most friendships are rooted in shared values and experiences. When we subscribe to the same views, we provide an anchor for one another and it brings us close.

But change brings disruption, and it's at this pivotal moment where we must decide whether (and how) we'll move forward together...or risk leaving someone behind. In these moments, we learn whether our friendship can stretch to make room for the new versions of ourselves, or if it won't be able to withstand the strain.

If you suddenly feel like everything between you and your friend has changed, here are some things to consider:

Possibility 1. She's experimenting.

Women are often criticized on both sides of their choices. If we choose to stay home with the kids, we're not ambitious enough; if we choose to work, then we are not maternal enough. If we wear clothes that reveal our shape, we are immodest, but if we cover up, we are prudes. If we are reserved, then we are shrinking ourselves, but when we speak loudly, we are not being ladylike. In a culture with such contradictory expectations of its women, we must be prepared to remake ourselves as we work to determine exactly who we'd like to be. Although your friend once pursued a certain type of man, enjoyed a certain kind of hobby, and adopted a particular set of beliefs, she will likely remake herself over and over.

Intellectually, we know our friends won't stay the same forever. But when it actually happens, it can be difficult to accept. The key is to not spiral into wondering what this change means for the friendship overall, jumping to assumptions that it signals the end. Instead, expect that she *will* change, and work to find ways you can relate to her in each new season.

Possibility 2. She's formed new priorities that shuffle the relationship.

One of the top friendship issues women bring to me during our session is struggling with change. They blame the other party for changing (or not changing enough), and it's difficult for them to identify or explain exactly how it happened.

I developed a concept known as The Priority Impact in an attempt to explain how personal changes come to manifest in our friendships.

There are three parts of *The Priority Impact Concept*: Choosing, Committing, and Prioritizing.

In the *choosing* stage, your friend begins making seemingly insignificant choices that may be inconsistent with her usual preferences and/or behavior. This may have no immediate impact on those around her.

When she makes these choices consistently over time, a new *commitment* is born. Eventually, to maintain the commitment, she must restructure her *priorities*. This includes finding new ways to redistribute her time, allocate her resources, and align her previous interests with her new demands.

Friends often feel the impact in this stage because connectedness in a relationship is deeply tied to these things.

If your friend chooses to become a mother, she is now committed to a certain lifestyle. And to maintain that lifestyle, she must rethink how she will spend the few hours she has available; how she'll disperse the money in her account; which goals she will release and pursue; and which worldviews will need updating to suit her new role.

By extension, the dynamics of her friendships will change.

Since this all begins with a few insignificant yet divergent choices, we will always be watching our friends shapeshift before our eyes. With your friend's new interests and priorities, you'll have to communicate your intention to stay connected, and work to find ways to move forward together.

What to Do

Response 1. Separate the branches from the root.

It's possible that only what you see on the surface of your relationship has changed, but the essence of what defines your friendship has not.

Write a list of the ways your friend is still herself, and how you will continue to relate to her in this new season. Then, write a list of how she's changed, along with the aspects of her changes that you can either accommodate or integrate into your own life.

Try not to fixate on the surface-level, circumstantial changes. Instead, keep your attention on the stuff that truly makes your friendship what it is.

Response 2. Practice parallel play.

When I was studying to become a teacher, I learned the concept of "parallel play," a form of play that young toddlers engage in. Children play *beside* one another, but not *with* one another. It may look like they're not involved, but they're observing and learning from one another.

Adults might benefit from this too.

There may be ways that we can engage in our own form of parallel play when a friend enters a world that's entirely foreign to us. If we're invested in the friendship but unclear about how to maintain our closeness when she begins to change, it's important to look for ways we can play beside each other without necessarily influencing each other (trying to get the other person to change, imposing our will).

Maybe this looks like literally joining her at the park and painting on your easel as she plays with her kids and you two catch up.

Or maybe your "parallel play" is less literal. Maybe the two of you now share different views on a hot political issue, so you agree to take that topic off the table when you get together and engage in activities you both enjoy, such as rock-climbing or a group fitness class.

How can you be alongside her without indulging with her? Shoulder to shoulder but not immersed? Whether she's a new convert, a new mom, newly sober—in what ways can you allow each other space to grow while staying connected?

Response 3. Create new memories.

It can be tempting to compare your present to the way things used to be. But the problem is the new season will never be able to live up to the idealized nostalgia of the past.

Comparing your solid past to your unfamiliar present may make you feel that the friendship is doomed because you can't imagine what the relationship looks like on the other side of these changes. Instead of longing for the memories you have of when you two were more in sync, get creative about ways you can create new memories. All your good times don't have to be in the past. Instead of sitting on the sidelines of her new lifestyle, find ways to make sure your paths cross.

Create something new together. Maybe you can finally take that mini road trip you've been talking about forever, or simply try the new wine bar that opened downtown. You could start a new show together or some other fun ritual—anything to help make sure you grow together. It will also make the "new version" of her not feel like such a stranger if you stay involved in each other's lives.

Response 4. Say the quiet part out loud.

Since we don't want to risk being perceived as jealous, disloyal, or close-minded, we often feign immediate support of a friend's new life. Whether she's getting married, having children, or going vegan (kidding! Kind of…), we pretend to understand her decision and act as if we are unaffected by the change.

But the truth is, we fear that our friendship will be impacted. We're sometimes confused by her choices and anxious about how it will affect the way we relate to one another. Will we spend less time together? Will she turn into someone we barely recognize?

Since we fail to share these concerns with our friend, we internalize them (or deny them altogether), and the friendship suffers at the hands of unresolved tension and unspoken fears.

But don't sit quietly on your worries.

Unpack the reasons it bothers you. What are you feeling? Are you scared you're losing her? Frustrated that you can't relate? Irritated that you feel judged? Excluded for not joining in?

Try this:

"Well, [new interest] isn't for me, but I love seeing how excited [new interest] makes you. Now (playfully), how do I make sure [new interest] doesn't suck you in so deeply that I don't get to see you anymore?"

or

"I gotta be honest: I'm torn because I'm so happy for you, but I'm also wondering what it means for us, because I just can't relate to that world. How can I make sure you feel supported while also staying true to my beliefs?"

Note: If the changes occurring in your friend's life put her (or others!) in danger, you need to speak up. Sometimes, we're reluctant to do this because we're scared we'll come across as judgmental and we're nervous that she won't respond well, but situations with severe consequences require a certain urgency.

Try this:

"Hey, I'm noticing [tangible observations you've made about her new life/behavior/beliefs], and I'm really worried about you. The last thing I want is for you to feel judged by me saying this, but I actually think I'd be a crappy friend if I stayed silent, and I know you'd do the same for me:

"I understand that people change, but these kinds of changes feel really dangerous. The [insert friend's name] I know wouldn't have been okay with this stuff a year ago, but the person I'm looking at today is very much okay with it, so I feel like I missed something.

"Help me understand what's going on, because I'm legitimately concerned."

Be warm while speaking directly, so that there's no confusion about how you feel. Ideally, you'll have a conversation that allows you to understand where she's coming from so you can have more accurate information to use in debunking problematic beliefs.

But if it seems like she won't let up, you'll have to lay out the terms. What does it mean for you and your friendship if she continues down this path? Will you have to "take some space" because it's difficult for you to put herself in this kind of danger? Are you prepared to call in reinforcements (whatever that looks like for you)? Do you want to set boundaries around what you two talk about? Help her understand what will happen if she continues to choose a path that you believe puts her in real harm. It's likely she'll be upset and indignant at first, but the hope is that she'll eventually come around.

When to Let Go

If your friend's new worldviews are a threat to your humanity, you may need to release the friendship in an act of self-preservation and respect. If she's formed new opinions or adopted a lifestyle that is in direct contrast to your identity or safety, you may decide it is too much—mentally or emotionally—to remain friends with someone who doesn't value the things that make you who you are.

You might also consider terminating a friendship if you find the changes exceed your willingness or capacity to adapt. If the very essence of your relationship is rooted in shared values and experiences but she pivots away from those core commonalities, you may not know how to remain bonded without them. This doesn't mean that you'll care for her any less, but you may decide that her changes decrease the overall satisfaction you get from the relationship. If this happens, it may not be worth it to you to invest in the same way. This does not make you a user or a fair-weather friend. But if your friend's changes are elemental and not just circumstantial, it is within your rights to determine whether you want to dedicate time (a limited resource!) into sustaining the relationship.

How to Know Whether You're the Newly Changed Friend

If recently you've been feeling that you no longer fit the spaces you once occupied, your friends may begin to experience you differently. If you find that you have an increased focus on the future instead of the past and you're not sure how your friendships will look in this next season, you may be in a time of change.

During your evolution, you may have friends who remind you of who you used to be or what you used to like. This is not a bad thing if you're a newly promoted career woman whose friends remind her of how she used to be at a job she hated where she wasn't paid well. They're pointing at your growth—to remind you of how far you've come—go, you!

But if you've decided to quit drinking to adopt a sober lifestyle yet your friends tell you used to be more fun when you drank, their "observations" are destructive. Consider distancing yourself from friends who prefer you to be in a space that was harmful to you.

You're the only person who can decide whether the changes you've made in your life are positive or negative, and the right friends will support any version of you that is growing in a healthy way. Look for those who show an ability and willingness to grant you the freedom to be your (new) self.

But show grace to those who hinder any changes you've identified as helpful and productive. While you might be the "newly changed" friend to others, it can be a positive thing. You'll just have to differentiate between the friendships that will be able to make the transition with you and those which were only meant for a season.

It's likely that, if your friends are slow to embrace your new change, it's simply because they miss the "you" that they're familiar with, and they're working to find ways to relate to this new version.

Here are a few phrases that sometimes trigger others and lead to resentment or misunderstanding during your transition:

"I've outgrown that/them..."
"I've evolved..."
"I don't have time for that stuff anymore..."

To be clear: There is nothing wrong with these phrases. But be aware of how you describe your past lifestyle to friends with whom you shared that history. If they're still in a particular season or still subscribing to beliefs that you've since released, consider how denouncing, belittling, degrading those behaviors/interests may be taken as you saying you're now "better" than them.

No, you can't control how other people feel. And context certainly matters here, but the general takeaway is to be mindful of conflating your new choices with choices that are "better" than theirs. How can you communicate your new mind-set without (intentionally) making others feel as if you believe you're in a superior place, and the life you once shared with them (that they still value) is inferior?

Try phrases like:

"I'm not in that place anymore..."
"That doesn't bring me joy anymore..."
"That's not the right path for me..."
"I'm just ready for something new..."

These phrases speak to the fact that you are making different choices, not necessarily better, superior choices. The key is to respect where your friends are, while also making attempts to invite them into the world if the friendships are ones that you want to maintain in your new life.

The Clingy Friend

I could tell that she felt guilty.

As she spoke with me about her friend Janet, Sarah—a successful thirty-five-year-old entrepreneur—grew increasingly more flustered. It was clear that she was conflicted about ending her friendship with Janet, and she was fretting about whether her desire to leave made her a "bad person."

When Sarah met Janet, she was looking for another "business friend" who would understand her lifestyle. She felt overwhelmed by her fast-paced lifestyle, and it was nice to finally meet someone who understood.

But their weekly chats turned into daily visits, and, while Sarah welcomed them at first, she gradually became overwhelmed by all that time together.

Janet had begun dropping by without calling, and Sarah was too passive to let her know that she wasn't okay with the unannounced drop-ins. Janet's incessant texting also became burdensome, and Sarah was struggling to keep up with the demand Janet's friendship put on her life.

When Janet and Sarah would hang out, Janet would spend the time talking about her long-term boyfriend and how uncaring he was. The chats sometimes lasted for hours into the evening, and then Janet was reaching out with a text again first thing the next morning.

"Even if we meet up to cowork, it's suffocating," Sarah confessed to me. "As soon as we get there, she's already asking about the next time we can get together. And then, she questions me about time that I spend with other friends. Like, damn! Stop pressing me!"

As Sarah spoke, her voice began to rise—it was obvious that she'd been sitting on this for a while.

"Sarah, I have to ask: Why are you reluctant to tell her that her expectations are too much for you? What are you afraid of?"

"Well," Sarah began, "if she didn't know how I felt before, she definitely knows now..."

It turns out that a week before our session, Janet was texting Sarah incessantly throughout the day. She didn't pick up on Janet's cues that she was busy, so Sarah stopped responding and texted her sister Natalie instead.

Exasperated, Sarah took a screenshot of Janet's messages and sent them to her sister with the message: *Look at this. She just won't quit. Why can't she take a hint?*

But that text never went to Sarah's sister.

Because she accidentally sent it to Janet.

Cringing, I asked Sarah what happened next.

"I mean, of course I felt awful," she admitted, averting her eyes. "I texted her apologizing for that and told her how wrong that was and how bad I felt. I was mortified."

Janet apologized for overwhelming her and promised to give her the space she needed.

"I'm so sorry things went down that way. Even though it wasn't ideal, was it effective? Is your friendship a bit more balanced now?"

"Nope," Sarah said hopelessly. "After a week, things went right back to how they were before."

Know the Signs

You may be dealing with a clingy friend if she:

- Calls and texts excessively
- Constantly needs reassurance
- Relies on you to validate her choices
- Feels threatened by your having other friends
- Searches for ways to spend as much time with you as possible
- Makes you feel burdened or overwhelmed

Getting Perspective

Healthy, mature friendship allows for each person to have a certain level of autonomy within the relationship. But when one friend becomes overly dependent on the other, it's a threat to each woman's personal freedoms.

The friendship may also suffer under the weight of resentment as one party begins to grow dissatisfied with unfair demands on her time, resources, and energy. She may begin to put distance between herself and the source of her stress, or she may feel obligated to meet each need, burning out in the process.

The goal of healthy friendships is interdependence, where each person depends on the other equally *while* maintaining a strong sense of self. But if one person is much more dependent on the other (not just for resources but for a sense of value and identity), it will strain the relationship over time because it's simply not sustainable.

Here are a few things to consider as you work to understand the dynamics with a needy friend:

Possibility 1. You give her something she needs.

Your friend may be overly dependent on your friendship because it meets a need she's not getting met elsewhere. Being with you may make her feel seen, loved, and important. You may be her primary source of companionship and entertainment. Being with you might make her feel safe.

Your friendship may be the only thing that offers her relief from pain, boredom, or feelings of insecurity.

In the case of my client Sarah, she told me that Janet admitted why she pursued their friendship so intensely: It turns out that Janet was living with her parents and her home was pretty dysfunctional—there was always tension in their home. She saw Sarah's home as an escape, a picture of the "loving" family she wanted for herself.

While we may empathize with our friend's reasons for clinging so strongly, it doesn't make her behavior any less overwhelming. But applying a more empathetic lens may help us to better understand where she's coming from.

Possibility 2. Your attachment styles are to blame.

If you have a friend with an anxious attachment style, it's possible that her care-givers were inconsistent in the ways that they provided attention and affection (or that she experienced this inconsistency in adult relationships!). You might notice that she has a frequent need for validation, seems uncomfortable being alone, and has an intense desire for intimacy or closeness. Your attention and reassurance are the remedy to her ongoing need to feel lovable and secure.

It's also possible that you *interpret* her as clingy because *you* have an avoidant attachment style. If you feel burdened when others need support, prioritize your needs over others', or have a tendency to ghost or withdraw, you might inter-pret a friend's reasonable attempts at connection with you as overwhelming.

(To learn more about how attachment styles affect our friendships, see Chapter 8.)

You'll be able to stir more compassion and understanding for your friend if you consider the ways in which her general anxiousness (or your avoidant tendencies) play a role in your dynamic.

Response 3. Her expectations simply aren't congruent with yours.

I frequently have women ask me about the "normal" amount of time between text exchanges and the "normal" amount of times two friends should hang out. My answer is always the same: it depends on the norms in your relationship.

Perhaps she expects that you contact each other every day while you think a weekly check-in is more reasonable. It's less about her being too demanding and more about your capacity and what you're able to man-age. Some friends are "high-touch," while others are more "low-touch." It's about finding compatibility.

You may believe your clingy friend to be objectively overwhelming, but the truth is that it's all relative. What's "too much" for you might be just enough for someone else. The trick is to recalibrate as a team by finding an arrangement that's manageable for everyone.

Although some people's needs are so extensive that you'll never be able to satisfy them, it's possible that your friend is willing to make adjustments if she learns about the impact of her expectations on the friendship.

Response 4. You need to feel needed.

While you may often find yourself irritated and inconvenienced by your friend's neediness, it's possible that you remain in the friendship because you have a desire to feel needed. If you deny your own needs to care for those of your friend; only feel useful when you're helping; and have few interests and commitments outside of your friend, you may be in a codependent relationship.

We often opt into friendships that reflect how we feel about ourselves. If you are a nurturer, you may attract people who need nurturing. If you consider yourself to be a natural giver, you might be surrounded by those who take. Be conscious of how much you immediately jump into the role of the "fixer," and how that tendency accounts for the type of people around you.

If you're neglecting your own needs to be perpetually attuned to your friend's needs, you may need to look for ways to either create more balance or completely remove yourself from the cycle.

Examine the ways in which the friendship serves you, then create (and enforce) firm boundaries to preserve your well-being.

What to Do

Response 1. Advocate for your preferences in real time.

Staying silent on an issue that bothers you will either lead to resentment or an inevitable blowup. Instead of withdrawing ("I'll just stop answering her texts and hope that she gets the point.") or attacking ("You text me way too much. It's really annoying!"), find a way to gently address each issue as it comes up.

If she texts you multiple times a day and then asks why you aren't responding, let her know what you prefer. Try this: *"I know you checked in with me a lot today, but I* prefer *to text after six p.m. when I'm home from work and have a chance to settle in."*

If she asks why you're spending time with other friends next weekend instead of hanging out with her, say: *"I only have so much free time, so I prefer to balance my weekends with seeing each of my friends so I can stay in touch with everyone."*

If your friend drops by your house without calling first, say: *"You know I love our hangouts, but I* prefer *when you let me know you're about to visit so I can make sure I'm not in the middle of something else and I can give you my full attention."*

Response 2. Focus on the objective, not the means.

To minimize your frustration, turn your attention from what she's doing and ask yourself *why* she's doing it.

Is it possible that she's texting you so often because, for her, that's a way of feeling connected throughout the day? When she gets jealous about you spending time with other friends, is it because she needs reassurance that she's not being replaced?

Feel free to ask her about her reactions to gain clarity, and then, where appropriate, offer reassurances to put her fears in perspective.

You: Why are you so upset by me spending time with other people?
She: *I just don't want you to start hanging out with them to the point where you don't hang out with me anymore.*
You: Our friendship offers me something totally different than what I get from them; you can't be replaced. I just want to spend equal time with everyone in my network.

Getting into the habit of zooming in on her intentions rather than her behavior can help you approach her from a place of empathy instead of annoyance.

Response 3. Examine the ways you may encourage her behavior.

Despite feeling overwhelmed by your friend's neediness, you may still be working to accommodate it. If she calls you several times throughout the day, you may roll your eyes but answer every call. When she makes you feel guilty about spending time with others, you may invite her to join you so that she doesn't feel lonely. If she seeks out your opinions on everything from which rug to buy to what she should wear, you may rack your brain to come up with solutions for every problem.

Whether your desire to meet her requests comes from a place of guilt or obligation, it only works to perpetuate the very behavior you don't like.

Response 4. Avoid telling her she is "too much."

I can't tell you how many women I've spoken with who can trace their insecurities back to a label they were given by a former friend. Whether they were told they were too loud, too dramatic, too friendly, too shy, or too needy, the labels made them shrink themselves for the next person, overthinking the ways in which they can be "less."

While you may genuinely be overwhelmed by your friend's clinginess, be sure to root your complaint in her behavior, not her character. The issue is her level of need not being in alignment with what you are able to give. While others may agree that she's too much, it's all still relative at the end of the day.

Whether you decide to address the matter or end the friendship altogether, the goal should be to do so while leaving as little damage as possible. You want to reconcile the division between you, not give her a complex about who she is.

Be specific about what's not working and come up with ways that the relationship dynamic can be more manageable for you.

When to Let Go

The complicated thing about loving a "clingy" friend is that it leaves you trying to balance your desire to support her with your need for autonomy. Reciprocity is a fundamental requirement of any healthy friendship, but if one person is required to show up more than the other (mentally, emotionally, financially), it creates an unhealthy imbalance.

If your friend is so reliant on you that it begins to take away from how you show up for others in your life (and your attempts to communicate this fail to inspire any meaningful change), you may consider ending the friendship.

If you've communicated your boundaries and preferences but she refuses to operate within them, you may need to release the relationship to protect your energy.

You should also examine whether she *expects* you to be responsible for her contentment. If she genuinely believes that your primary role in the friendship is to be the source of her wholeness and stability, there will never be a point where you're released from those obligations.

And finally, try to identify your reasons for staying in the friendship. Is it out of a sense of obligation or duty? Do you fear that you'd look like you're abandoning her if you ended the relationship (and you don't want to be perceived as disloyal, a highly valued female trait in our culture)? If you find that you're staying because leaving would make you look or feel bad, reconsider the purpose of the friendship and release it if your main reason for staying isn't healthy.

How to Know Whether You're the Clingy Friend

If friends do not explicitly tell us that we're being clingy, it may be hard to recognize it on our own. But you might be too dependent on your friendships if you're the main person initiating, you experience intense feelings of rejection when they're unavailable, and when you become increasingly dependent on their approval and validation.

You should also examine attitudes you've adopted about friendship overall, and how they may be impacting how you show up: Do you believe that friends are responsible for your happiness? Do you believe that if you have friends then you don't need a therapist? If you subscribe to the idea that other people should be the source of your joy and security and should offer all the solutions to your problems, you may want to reexamine your definitions and expectations of friendship. Friendship is essential, yes, but the healthiest friendships also encourage each person to maintain a sense of self.

If you don't know where to start, ask yourself what a more "secure" person would do: What assumptions would they make if a friend doesn't return a text or answer the phone? What thoughts would they have when they see a friend spending time with other people? What would they do when a friend is unavailable to spend time together? This can help you regain a sense of balance.

It also helps to ask yourself what evidence a friend has already given you that she cares about you. Hold tightly to these facts whenever you begin to feel jealous, worried, or controlling.

Consider investing in other friendships that allow you to build a more well-rounded network (so that you're not entirely relying on one single person in your life) and lean in to personal interests that you can enjoy independently to develop a stronger sense of self.

While we certainly benefit from having friends who we can spend time with and rely on for support, they should not become our sole source of joy, entertainment, or security.

The Negative Friend

You have eighteen minutes left until your lunch break is over, so you eat the last of your sandwich while mindlessly scrolling on your phone. Just as you're about to comment a "heart eyes" emoji on your friend's latest puppy post, you get a call.

Natasha's name flashes across the screen, and an icy dread fills your chest. With a deep sigh, you begin to weigh the pros and cons of silencing the call: On one hand, it could be a genuine emergency. What if she needs you for something important and you don't come through?

But it's also possible that this is going to be yet another long vent session. She'll hold you hostage as she outlines every detail of her latest crisis, filled with remarks about how much she hates her job...and her family... and her apartment.

When you first began dodging her calls, you felt guilty. She's a good friend and you share a ten-year history together. But lately it's become too much—her relentless griping and complaining leave you exhausted, and you just can't do it anymore.

But you can only avoid her for so long before she demands to know what's going on.

How do you tell her that her negativity is wearing you out? You'd like to think of yourself as a loving and supportive friend, but her tendency to hijack every conversation with a pessimistic rant is more than you can handle.

You want to show up for her, but how are you supposed to love a friend who brings you down?

Know the Signs

Here are a few signs that you're dealing with a negative friend:

- She *frequently* vents about troubles she's having with things like work, family, or relationships.
- You've begun silencing her calls and making excuses not to link up as much as usual.
- You've adopted the role of the "therapist" and feel pressured to help solve her problems.
- After spending time together, you feel mentally and emotionally depleted.
- You're complaining more than usual whenever you're in her company.

Getting Perspective

The difference between productive and unproductive venting and complaining is *purpose.*

If we're venting to get "unstuck" and find clarity on something, it can be helpful.

But when we express dissatisfaction just for the sake of being negative—or when we're incessantly ruminating about something that's annoying us—it can be overwhelming and unproductive.

When your friend is venting, does she ultimately get to a place where she's ready to move forward? Or does she seem to be stuck in a continuous negativity loop that she doesn't want to leave despite your attempts to help? Researchers[57] refer to these people as "help-rejecting complainers."

When we fall into the habit of highlighting all the things we don't like, it's not only unproductive, but it can be physically, mentally, and emotionally destructive.

Research[58] finds that when people complain with a purpose, they're happier than those who complain for complaining's sake. And people in this second group can become a major turn-off to friends.

It can be challenging to support a friend during her distress while preserving your own mental health. And "secondhand stress" is a thing.

When we see someone showing signs of anxiety, we experience the same negative emotions, and the closer you are to someone, the greater the impact.[59] For example, if your best friend is displaying negative emotions, your levels of cortisol will rise higher than they would if you witnessed the same behavior from a stranger.

Our brain has something called "mirror neurons" that allow us to mimic the emotions and actions of others, and this is why some of us leave an interaction with a negative friend feeling so emotionally and cognitively depleted.

So, how do we work with a friend whose complaining has crossed the line from casual to chronic?

Instead of writing your friend off as "too negative," first try to understand what may be driving her behavior.

Possibility 1. Her brain is on autopilot.

Research[60] has found that the more we complain, the easier our brain makes it for us to do.

Here's how it works: When you repeat a behavior consistently, your brain's neurons begin to stretch toward one another in an effort to transfer information faster. It's as if they're saying, "Hey, it looks like we're going to be doing this a lot, so let's make it easier to talk to one another!"

This means that if your friend's an OG complainer who's been in the game for a while, then it's almost second nature for her to find fault in any person or situation. It becomes a reflex, and without her even realizing it, her brain's been set to autopilot.

If you have a friend who has a gift of complaining about anything, it's likely because she's been practicing for so long. The good news is that people who have this habit often aren't aware of how bad it is. If she's told what's happening and willing to adopt a more positive outlook, then there may be hope for her (and your friendship!).

Possibility 2. You (unintentionally) encourage her.

Complainers thrive on "amens," so when you validate her grievances with responses like, "Yeah, I agree," "Me too," or "That's so true," you're encouraging more of the same.

If she's always in the habit of criticizing her looks, be mindful of the ways you talk about your own appearance.

If your friend's constantly venting about her troubles (her job, appearance, or relationships) be careful about the way you jump into therapist mode, jumping at the chance to solve her issues. When the majority of our interactions take on a client-patient dynamic, it can become burdensome to the friend who's expected to be the counselor.

Reflect on the ways you may unintentionally validate and encourage her negativity, because it may be signaling to her that you're a sympathetic audience.

Possibility 3. Social media has a grip on her.

If your friend's negativity is mostly centered on low self-esteem and body image, consider the role that social media plays in her life.

How much time does your friend spend on social media? Several studies have found that frequent use of certain social media platforms leads to depression and appearance anxiety, and that those who engage in social comparison are most at risk for the negative outcomes that are associated with social media use.

The dissatisfaction she feels about her appearance is likely because there's a gap between what she sees and what she views as ideal. These ideals could have been fed to her by critical caregivers or by social media, with its endless (edited!) images that make us wish for a better complexion, bigger breasts, and a flatter stomach.

Because she's uncomfortable in her own skin, she may reject your compliments, make self-deprecating comments, or become obsessed with posting on social media to get likes.

When your friend speaks poorly of herself, try responding with phrases like, "I wish you saw yourself the way I see you." You might also try engaging her by asking, "What would it take for you to finally genuinely accept yourself for who you are?" or encourage her to lean in to the things that do make her feel good about herself.

What to Do

Once you've gained a bit of perspective on your friend's behavior, you might be ready to take action. Here are a few strategies to try:

Response 1: Package your boundary as a favor.

If there is one particular subject that really gets your friend worked up, find a way to let her know that it's off-limits...for her sake.

Try this:

"Girl, I feel bad because talking about [insert subject here] always gets you really worked up, and I don't want you so stressed out. So, how about we talk about [insert new subject here] for a while instead?"

or

If she is venting about something for the hundredth time, listen, and then after a brief pause, say, *"Well, I'm sorry to hear that's not going well. And I can tell it frustrates you. How about this—tell me something good! What's going well for you right now?"*

or

"When we link up, we spend most of the time talking about the things that aren't going well. I'm realizing that I don't know enough about what's going right in your life. What can we celebrate?"

or

If your friend's negativity centers on her own flaws and perceived shortcomings, you can try offering something like, *"Hey, I can't let you talk about my friend like that."*

To be clear, you would only use this for the friend whose complaints have become chronic and persistent, despite your attempts to help.

This is a way of validating her frustration while also offering her a chance to shift her focus to something that may be more uplifting. She may view this as a favor to her, as you work to draw her away from the subject that gets her so agitated. This is a good approach for temporary, momentary issues.

Response 2: Offer to tag-team a solution.

Research from Stanford University reveals that chronic complaining shrinks the part of your brain that's responsible for critical thinking and problem-solving. If your friend has been complaining long enough, she's literally made it more difficult to create solutions for the problems she's venting about. This creates an endless cycle of her complaining incessantly with no end in sight.

And while we sometimes need to vent to process, not problem-solve, it can become detrimental if we engage frequently over time. It's especially dangerous because women tend to engage in "co-rumination"—rehashing an issue over and over—to bond with one another. But studies show that this increases cortisol, the stress hormone. Listening to (and joining in on) our friend's daily vent sessions are harmful, so finding solutions is the way out.

If she was looking for you to empathize with her hundredth complaint, it may stop if she sees that you aren't willing to engage. And if she responds to your attempts to help with something like, "Well, I just want to vent right now," try this:

"You know that when you need support, I'm your girl. But this situation has taken so much of your joy, and I'm ready to think through ways we can solve this

problem instead of rehashing things, because at this point, I don't think that's doing either one of us any good."

You can be firm when her negativity has become harmful. Hopefully, she'll respect your attempts to uplift her.

Best-case scenario: she works with you to find a solution to her problems, and those problems go away.

Worst-case scenario: she stops bringing her complaints to you because you won't entertain them.

Win-win.

Response 3. Refer her to someone who can help.

When your friend begins to complain about the same thing she always does and you've already tried each of the preceding strategies, it may be time to let her know that someone else may be better suited to help.

You can either refer her to a professional *or* anyone in her life who's qualified to help. For example, if she's always talking about her job, encourage her to speak with Human Resources. If she's always talking about her sister, encourage her to collaborate with her mother to address her sister's issues. If she's talking about her marriage, point to another one of her friends who's married and may be able to offer more perspective.

Try this:

"You've mentioned this to me a few times now and I want to support you, but I don't think I'm qualified to help much. Why don't you talk to [name of more qualified person], because she can probably give more guidance than I can."

Although you may be frustrated, the key to this approach is to deliver your suggestion gently and genuinely, without sarcasm. It's very possible that speaking with someone qualified to help won't just end the complaining, but address the root issue of her aggravation. Phrasing things this way puts you in the role of "helper" and removes you from the obligations of "counselor."

When to Let Go

Positivity is a critical component of any meaningful friendship. If being together isn't a pleasurable experience, why would we even elect to build more together?

Being positive doesn't mean we avoid talking about difficult things. But when we take an aerial view of our friendship, we can determine whether the majority of our interactions are pleasurable or pessimistic.

In fact, a study by John Gottman revealed that the "magic ratio" of positive to negative interactions necessary to maintain a happy and stable relationship is 5 to 1.[61] This means that, for every one negative interaction you have, you need five positive interactions to keep things happy overall. Consider the last few interactions you had with your negative friend. How many of those left you feeling drained and defeated afterward? If the ratio is pretty high, it speaks to the overall experience of the friendship.

At the risk of oversimplifying things, think about whether the good times outweigh the bad. Sure, you all have a lot of fun memories and she is a caring person. But if her venting and complaining leave you feeling drained most of the time (and she's unwilling to make adjustments), you may need to release the friendship.

Also, consider who *you* are before, during, and after your interactions:

Before: Anxious; dreading the hangout; avoiding calls and texts
During: Feeling stressed; more irritable and critical than normal
After: Exhausted; feeling guilty about joining your friend in her
    negativity (which you now understand to be contagious)

Think about who you are when the two of you are together. Do you complain more than you normally would when you're with her? Do you become more irritable and critical than normal?

If you find the need to minimize your achievements, make self-deprecating comments, or take on the burden of her ongoing discontent, question the ways in which the friendship is impacting your own well-being.

Note: It's not uncommon to feel guilty when you end a friendship with a negative friend. A part of you might feel responsible for her happiness, and if you're the only person in her life that she can talk to, you might feel that you're abandoning her. Try to remember that while friendships have their challenges, *healthy* friendships won't deplete you of your joy and energy.

How to Know Whether You're the Negative Friend

It's easy to fall into a habit of complaining, but the key is to become aware and then commit to "rewiring" your brain by focusing on seeing the positive (and yes, as clichéd as that sounds, it's true).

Here are a few signs that you may be known as the "negative" friend:

- Friends either go silent or change the subject after you go on a long rant.
- Most of your conversations center on the things going wrong more than the things going right.
- When friends offer solutions to your problems, you respond with, "Yeah, but...," listing ways those solutions probably won't work for you.
- You don't know what you'd talk to your friends about if you weren't allowed to vent negative emotions.

If you've been called out for being negative, try cultivating an attitude of gratitude. When you feel like complaining, shift your attention to something that you're grateful for. Research conducted at the University of California, Davis,[62] found that people who worked daily to cultivate an attitude of gratitude are more satisfied with their lives overall. Any time you experience negative or pessimistic thoughts, use this as a cue to shift gears and to think about something positive. In time, a positive attitude will become a way of life.

No one is saying you can't vent with your friends, but take the time to reflect on how much of your friendship leans that way overall.

Also consider other outlets to help you process your grievances. Journaling, therapy, and spiritual support are all ways to help you make sense of where you are. While one benefit of friendship is to have people we can bring our troubles to, we must also look for ways to build a toolkit of self-care and community care to help us through.

While this is something you want to nurture for your own well-being, it will also position you for better friendships, because people with a more positive outlook on life often make better friends overall.[63]

Part Three

LETTING GO AND STARTING AGAIN

Chapter 6

How to Write Your "Comeback" Story

You know the feeling well.

It used to be so easy, so natural in the beginning. But after having a conflict with a friend, it can be hard to spend time together without comparing the tensions of the present to the simple comfort of the past. Should you just pretend that it never happened? Do you have (another) difficult talk? Would things be easier if you let the friendship go? It feels like things would be easier if you didn't have so many conflicting emotions—sure, you still enjoy your friend's company, but you're also considering whether it would be better to create a little distance.

But sometimes that "space" is the beginning of the end.

So, what are you supposed to do when you're straddling both sides of the fence?

First, you're going to have to get clear about how you want to move forward. Because it turns out that maintaining these kinds of mixed feelings may be detrimental to your health. A study by Julianne Holt-Lunstad[64] found that while ambivalent friendships share some of the same qualities as "primarily positive" friendships, they aren't as good for your health. While friendships that are positive and supportive offer a host of health benefits, those with a mix of positive and negative feelings are associated with high blood pressure and anxiety.

The sooner we determine how we want to proceed with a friend after friction, the sooner we can enjoy peace of mind.

Renegotiating the Terms

In a season of friendship conflict, it's tempting to go straight to thoughts like:

I can't believe she's so inconsiderate.
I have no idea who she is anymore.
How in the world could she think that's an acceptable thing to say to me?

But it might help to stop and facilitate a moment to think about the data that you're getting from the situation—about you, your friend, and your relationship itself, specifically with regards to boundaries.

It's hard to scroll social media for three seconds without seeing a video about setting boundaries. It's become a hot topic, but there are many elements of the public discourse that gloss over the unsexy bits on this subject.

The truth is, most of us aren't able to articulate our boundaries until they're crossed. Something happens and then we're immediately overwhelmed by feelings of rage or unease. Suddenly, we know that something is wrong and our sense of safety needs to be restored.

Moments of conflict tend to reveal:

An emergence of new boundaries: Conflict sometimes reveals new boundaries. Maybe we didn't know that we were sensitive to a subject until a new friend introduces it into conversations. Maybe we don't know we're triggered by something until a friend oversteps. When a friend's words or actions cause us to bristle, it points to a sensitive area that needs protecting, and the conflict ultimately informs us of how to act.

The need for personal recommitments: Sometimes, our discomfort is the result of making internal compromises. It's worth asking ourselves how much of the conflict we're experiencing is because of our personal choice to let things go too far. We have to ask ourselves whether we're attributing our own lack of discipline to the external situations that involve our friends.

A need to make our boundaries known: Self-awareness is a critical part of being able to communicate what you need. If a friend's behavior is triggering you (whether she means to or not!), you'll have to make it known. You're not being confrontational or dramatic.

Expressing your boundaries is like giving your friends a page from the handbook on how to love you well. The right people will welcome this data and be relieved that there are fewer guessing games on how to show up for you. They can now operate with confidence when you're together because they have a better understanding of what makes you feel safe. They are liberating, not restrictive.

A moment for renegotiation: Maybe what worked for your friendship before doesn't work anymore. The unspoken agreement you once had with friends to show up in a certain way may not fit as you grow. But we fall into a rhythm with our friends, and before long, the relationship's ecosystem functions on autopilot; but as time passes, you'll begin to be stretched in new ways that required a different "setting."

The falling-out you're having with a friend might be data you need to know that things shifted over time, and you'll need to make the proper adjustments to keep things on track.

How to Set "Affirmative Boundaries"

So much of the discussion around boundaries makes it seem that we must firmly and loudly list the things we won't tolerate. We come to new friendships with our rule book in hand, ready to call out each infraction. But if boundaries are about showing friends how to love us well, we can achieve the same goal by providing illustrations of what we want, rather than emphasizing what we don't.

When we finally muster the courage to express our boundaries, we often do it in a way that makes the other party feel as if they're being rejected. While we can't take responsibility for others' feelings, there are things we can do to minimize offense and increase connection.

Affirmative boundaries involve packaging your "no" as a "yes." The underlying message is the same, but instead of your friend hearing what she *can't* do and you *won't* tolerate, you'll share what you *do* want while affirming the relationship.

Examples:

- Instead of saying, "I won't tolerate your calling me at late hours," try "I'm most alert and attentive on the phone before eight p.m., so that's when I'd prefer to catch up." Then, stop answering her late-night calls.
- Instead of saying, "I don't like when you're late," try "Hey, I love when we both get here on time so I can get as much time with you as possible! When you're running behind, it makes me anxious while I'm waiting, and I want to make sure we start our hangouts with me being in the right headspace!" Then, consider how you'd like to physically respond to her lateness.
- Instead of "Don't talk to me with an attitude!" you might try "I respond best when you talk to me the way you did last night. I've noticed I'm more receptive when our disagreements have that kind of tone." Then, decide (and articulate) how you'll respond the next time you feel that she's approaching you disrespectfully.

Now, depending on your personality, you might be thinking, *Danielle, I don't have time for all of that—I like to make it plain!* I hear you! Look for various ways that you can craft an affirming message. Maybe your words are direct, but your tone is light. Maybe your tone is stern, but your body language still communicates warmth (e.g., touching her gently on the hand while playfully saying, "Girl, you gotta stop being late! Waiting for you in the parking lot stresses me out!").

This creates a space for your friend to receive your message as an invitation to love you well instead of an accusation of all the ways she's not measuring up.

After communicating, you'll have to practice upholding. You would do this by letting your friend know what you will do the next time she pushes you past your comfort zone.

Try something like:

"Paige, I'd love to come to your barbecue next weekend! But I'm telling you now: if there are little comments about my not drinking and people start to make jokes or pressure me, I'll have to leave. I just don't want it to come as a surprise, so I wanted to give you a heads-up now."

If Paige begins to pressure you after being repeatedly reminded and made aware of the consequences, you'll have to assess how much Paige values your emotional safety, and determine how to move forward with her friendship, should you choose to maintain the relationship. But following through on your consequences shows friends the impact their behavior has on you, and encourages them to self-correct so they can keep you in their lives at your optimal levels of well-being.

Amanda E. White is an author, therapist, and founder of the Therapy for Women Center (and creator of the popular Instagram account @therapyforwomen). She often speaks to clients about boundary-setting in an effort to help them understand how to do it in a healthy way.

"Typically, setting the boundary is not what makes the boundary. It's the *maintenance* of a boundary over time. Some of us have unrealistic expectations—we have to remember that people are human, and they may forget. It doesn't mean they're actively trying to piss you off or hurt you just because they don't do exactly what you want them to do."

Amanda suggests using a "soft start" that assumes positive intentions. "Openers like 'I know you didn't mean it...' or 'I know you have good intentions...' assume they love you and let them know that you know they care. It's a soft start that can be more helpful than labeling them in a negative way, which would make anyone defensive because *they* don't see themselves that way."

You'll have to be prepared to give little reminders (depending on the violation), because your friends are likely operating according to habits they've been working with for years. Or they may be doing things that other people in their lives allow (or encourage!) them to do.

If a friend reacts to your reminder with, "Oh, sorry! I know you feel uncomfortable when I do that—I forgot. But I'll be sure to remember next time!" she's demonstrating her intentions to self-correct. But if she is indignant, offended, or minimizing, it points to a lack of respect for your emotional safety.

In the end, it may simply require you to measure your margin. How much space do you give friends to make mistakes? The key is to courageously voice your needs while remaining aware of your shortcomings as you compassionately extend grace to your friends.

We know that there must be a margin for error, because we're all going to make mistakes. In any human relationship, we will cross the line and disappoint each other. And we won't always be the offended party.

Sometimes, we'll find ourselves on the side of the offender. And it helps to know how to restore trust and make amends.

The Art of Apologizing

Despite our best efforts to reconcile after a transgression, it can be difficult to move forward without an apology. And apologies can be complicated. Depending on who you are, you either withhold them to avoid an admission of defeat or offer them in excess because you never want anyone to be mad at you.

Both approaches do little to offer reassurance to the injured party that we understand where she's coming from and genuinely care—which, let's be honest, is all that they really want.

If the idea of saying "I'm sorry" makes your heart race, you're not alone.

Apologizing can feel like an admission that the friendship is less than perfect. Conflict can feel like the beginning of the end, so we might find ourselves withholding an apology to somehow delay or avoid a penalty.

And let's be honest: Apologizing can make us feel really vulnerable. When we're a part of a culture that continually tells us to be strong, apologizing can feel like a weakness. So, it requires a reframe, because it's not that we're losing our "power." But we do have to give over trying to control the situation, trusting that our friend knows our heart, assumes good intention, and wants to restore harmony.

When Defensiveness Delays the Process

Our brain works so hard to keep us whole. So, when we hear that someone thinks we're flawed, weak, offensive, uncaring, or dishonest—essentially, anything other than perfect—we go into "protection mode." When we're scared of being rejected, we might instinctively try to balance the scales by reaching for the following (unhealthy) tactics:

- Defensiveness ("I'm not wrong, you are!")
- Blaming ("I only did that because of what you said.")
- Indignation ("I can't believe you're actually upset!")
- Self-victimizing ("I guess I just can't do anything right!")
- Gaslighting ("I don't think I actually *said* that…")
- Giving the silent treatment (not speaking; giving one-word responses)
- Attacking the "accuser" ("Wait, *you're* the one who…")

But here's the thing: These responses only exacerbate the tension between you and the friend who's calling you out. If she's communicating pain or discomfort (whether it be in the form of anger, sadness, or gentle, matter-of-fact references), *she just expressed a need.* Your most immediate response might be to justify your actions or to distract from being in the hot seat, but these moments—while deeply uncomfortable—are unlikely opportunities for connection.

Then, remember that apologizing is not about admitting defeat and surrendering to our friend, the "victor." It's not a power struggle. It's not a game.

Apologizing is about showing the injured party that you care.

A Humble Path to Reconnection

Molly McPherson is a nationally recognized expert in crisis public relations management, and the author of *Indestructible: Reclaim Control and Respond with Confidence in a Media Crisis.*[65] Brand leaders turn to her when they're in trouble and want to preserve or recover their reputation.

In a nutshell, she makes a living from helping people apologize the right way:

"Apologizing can be difficult for anyone, whether it's in a friendship or as the face of a PR crisis. When you lose trust in someone, it's even worse. Conflicts usually arise from a loss of trust between two people. Betraying that trust can be costly if you get the apology wrong. If it's your public image, the cost may be financial; it's a friendship, you risk losing someone you care about."

Molly offers three key components of a solid, sincere apology:

1. *Own up to your mistakes.* "Apologize sincerely to anyone you have hurt. Acknowledging your wrongdoings and accepting responsibility for the pain you may have caused demonstrates humility and a genuine desire to make things right." This is important because it also shows that her feelings actually matter to you.

2. *Explain what happened.* "Sharing details about the rift can provide some context to the situation, but do not get too comfortable and start blaming your friend. Make sure you stick to the facts." Context is good, but you should also express concern and sympathy if you have hurt your friend. You can also look for opportunities to explain how your actions don't match your values.

3. *Make a promise.* "Next time, you're going to do something differently, and then you'll have to follow through." Explain how you plan to proceed in the future and the steps you'll take to make amends.

Try to be sincere in your tone and body language when you tell your friend what you're going to do better going forward. A relationship's future often depends on two things: accountability and an apology when someone messes up.

Hopefully from there, you can both let it go.

Moving Forward Together

Once you've worked through your initial conflict, consider exactly what you need to move forward together as friends. Some women jump immediately to the option of terminating the friendship (most often through a gradual fading out), but it's because they aren't aware of their other options. If you value the friendship but aren't sure how to keep the friendship going after it's been strained by a blowup, here are some ideas.

The first thing you might consider is "recategorizing" your friends. This method privately alters how you classify a friendship. Maybe you had her as a top-tier ride-or-die friend, the one you shared everything with. But if your friendship's changed after a conflict, you might need to adjust your expectations so you're not consistently disappointed in the way that she shows up.

Maybe you all still hang out and talk to each other, but you make an internal decision to be more discerning about what you share. Maybe you find a way to accept that she's less available and enjoy her companionship when you can in the ways that you can. Maybe she's not able to provide adequate emotional support in the way that you would like, so you find a way to be content with the other ways that she contributes to your life.

This doesn't make you less loyal or committed. This doesn't mean it's a "fake" friendship. It just means that you care enough about her to experiment with the kind of dynamics that will help your friendship thrive.

It might seem like you're settling, but think about the ways that friendship can exist on a continuum. It can be quite an adjustment to engage in the friendship in a new way, but if we become "all or nothing" about what friendship looks like after conflict, we're going to leave a lot of good relationships prematurely. Things might not look the way they did before, but the friendship might still bring value to our lives.

While recategorization might be a permanent adjustment in some friendships, others see it as a temporary season that's necessary to return to each other with more healing and perspective.

And this, my friends, is known as a "fake back."

The "Fake Back"

A "fake back "is the awkward period where you continue to engage with a friend without the same rhythm and comfort you had in the "before times." While some see this as a sign that the friendship is over, others accept it as a prerequisite to finding each other again.

In Issa Rae's hit show *Insecure*, best friends Molly and Issa navigate the challenges of adulthood in Los Angeles. During the third season, they struggle to maintain their friendship amidst respective changes in their careers and love lives, and tensions rise.

Everything comes to a head in season four when a series of misunderstandings and unspoken emotions lead to verbal sparring so hurtful that it almost gets physical. When the episode aired, the online discourse that followed became heated as viewers debated who was "in the wrong" and shared their views about whether friends could (or should) reconcile after such a hostile falling-out.

When season five debuted, Issa and Molly are trying to get back into a rhythm, but it's…awkward. Despite their best efforts to be cool again, it just feels unnatural.

In one scene, Issa talks to her friend Kelli. She asks Kelli how long it took for things to get back to normal after a falling-out with *her* bestie, Tiffany.

"Oh, God. We were 'fake back' before we were *back* back. I mean, child, the jokes I laughed at wasn't even funny. Just don't force it, you know? It'll happen when it happens. Just keep being there for her. Like, what does she need right now?"

I know you've been here too.

Both women try their best to move forward, but it's hard to pretend that there isn't residual tension from the conflict they had a few weeks (months?) earlier. It feels strange to try to still be operating from muscle memory with clumsy chemistry. It's so tempting to just back off, because being together is a reminder of how things have changed. It's natural to want to pull away from uncomfortable spaces, and sometimes, we really do need a break to figure out how we feel and to look at our situation with fresh perspective.

Once we get clarity, we return to a friendship that has even more love and respect than before.

I've seen a lot of friendships die in the "fake back" stage. But it helps to continually remind ourselves that one day, we'll catch our rhythm again—as long as we keep showing up.

The Friendship Cycle: Sam and Crystina's Story

Crystina met her best friend Sam in the sixth grade. The girls became incredibly close over the next few years and even attended the same college.

During their junior year, they decided to move in together. Suddenly, they had front-row seats to the intimate details of the other's daily life.

Sam had a long-term boyfriend that Crystina couldn't stand, and while it may have been an issue that was easy to avoid before moving in together, it had now become an undeniable fixture in their conversations. Sam and her boyfriend had extreme highs and lows, and Crystina was very verbal in her disapproval of their relationship. The issue caused mounting friction in their friendship.

While Sam was committed to staying with her boyfriend, Crystina was very much single.

"During that season of my life, I felt empowered in owning my sexuality. But little did I know, Sam very much judged me for it."

After a night of drinking, the two girls got into yet another argument about Sam's boyfriend. Sam stormed off and went into the garage, where she began venting about Crystina to her sister. Tired of feeling the weight of Crystina's judgment, she exploded, calling her a "whore" and talking about her sleeping around.

Crystina overheard everything.

"I followed her into the garage and when she saw me, she froze. And I just stood there. I remember feeling sick to my stomach, and honestly, for the first time, I was speechless."

She returned to her room heartbroken, angry, and embarrassed.

The next morning, Sam went to Crystina's room to apologize. She'd felt terrible for the things she said, but the damage was done. For the remainder of the year that they lived together, they never fully discussed the incident. They stopped confiding in each other, and when their lease was up, they chose to live with other people.

But they worked together at the same company and had several mutual friends, so it was hard to completely pull away. The friend group never picked a side in Sam and Crystina's situation. Instead, they encouraged them to rekindle their friendship, saying things like, "You guys love each other. You need to work it out."

Crystina: "In the years that followed, we talked about it. It was a series of conversations over time, and there were even a few more arguments. Sam continued to express that she felt bad, and I wanted to forgive her. But I knew that internally I wouldn't be able to trust her for a while."

It took a long time, but the girls eventually worked it out.

Their conversations led to a greater understanding and a renegotiation of terms: if they wanted to preserve their friendship, they'd need new boundaries.

Crystina agreed to keep her commentary about Sam's relationship to a minimum. "I know myself back then. I said things all the time that were a little jarring, I was never perfect." She saw the impact it had on their friendship and didn't want Sam to feel judged, defensive, or unsupported. So, she stopped criticizing Sam's relationship and allowed her to make her own choices without trying to influence them.

"We learned that—for both of us—the less judgement you have on another person's relationships, the easier it is for your friendship."

Crystina says that despite the years of tension and emotional distance, there was always an underlying "sense of family." Even though they weren't speaking as much, she always knew they'd bounce back.

"The thing about friendship is that you have to be forgiving. You can't just cut someone off after one big fight. In all other facets of our friendship, Sam had always been there. Always. So, at the end of the day, it was worth sticking it out."

Crystina says that when she looked over the history of the relationship and remembered the major life milestones they'd been through (the death of family members, breakups, marriages), it was a reminder of what she was fighting for: a friendship filled with love and support.

"Conflict would not tear us apart. We've been through quite a bit. Cutting each other off just wasn't an option. And I don't know how we managed to get past that point. Part of it is that I'm a forgiving person. I don't like holding grudges, or having people mad at me. I want to work it out immediately, and she's like that too. Plus, we're overcommunicators. So, it was those things in conjunction with not wanting to throw away so many years of friendship."

Despite the years of distance and disappointment, putting in the work toward reconciliation brought them closer than before.

"Now it feels like there's nothing we can't work through. If we argue now, it's sisterly in that we fight but we love hard. The gloves are off. The walls are down.

"She can't really hide her thoughts from me and I can't hide mine from her. And why should we? We've been friends for so long that there should only be honesty between us. And if there isn't anything but honesty, then it won't end well."

Although it had been a rocky road, Crystina and Sam's friendship survived (and deepened), because they allowed time, humility, and intention to bring them back together.

This story illustrates the power of owning up to mistakes, being vulnerable, and taking space to be able to forgive and proclaim a desire to move forward—all parts of a friendship game plan that Molly McPherson would approve of.

"If you have accountability—whether it's in business or in personal relationships—people are more likely to give you grace and help you get back on your feet. Because as much as people tear each other down, people *love* a comeback story."

Chapter 6 Questions

1. Can you think of a situation you've had with a friend that could have been resolved sooner if someone offered an apology?
2. How comfortable do you feel setting boundaries with your friends?
3. After having "friction" with a friend, how difficult is it for you to recover?

Chapter 7 Preview Question

Have you ever ended a friendship? If so, how did you do it?

Moving On Without Her

When you're trying to figure out whether to let a friend go, it can be really stressful. Weighing the freedoms and consequences of terminating a friendship can be confusing. Sure, you're ready to release the frustration and anxiety that come with maintaining a friendship that no longer feels good, but you're also painfully aware of the drama and guilt that might ensue.

Many women would argue that friendship breakups are more difficult than romantic ones, and I agree. There are so many personal and cultural factors that make these situations seem so uniquely painful.

Unlike romantic relationships, we don't consider the possibility of a breakup when we begin entertaining each other. With childhood mantras like "best friends forever" and "friends for life," it seems ridiculous to consider the end at the beginning. So, when a friendship *does* end, we struggle to reconcile reality with our expectations.

When things don't work out with someone we're dating, we can easily reduce the situation to simply not being each other's type. But with friends, it feels like a rejection of who we are at the core. With friends, we come to believe we are funny, interesting, desirable, and worthy of love, and we can point to their decision to befriend us as evidence of that. So, when *friends* "unchoose" us, it can make us question who we are and what we have to offer. When it's over, it comes as a huge blow to our self-esteem.

And when we end things with a friend who's deeply integrated into our social lives, the breakup feels especially disruptive. The absence leaves us more vulnerable than we expected as we suddenly have nothing to do after work or on the weekends—at least, not without our best girl. Social outings feel pointless when we can't share the experience with the friend we've lost.

During the friendship, it's comforting to have someone who knows us so well. But we see the risk of that kind of intimacy when things are over. It's common to feel fearful and powerless as she reenters the world with knowledge of our most personal parts. She's been a witness to our trials and triumphs—she's seen sides of us that no one else knows. Then suddenly she leaves with that intel and those memories and it can leave us feeling anxious and exposed.

In a word, it's...complicated.

And maybe that's why some of us stay much longer than we should. When we break up with a friend, we're not just parting with the bad stuff. We're losing the good stuff too.

Signs to Let Go

Despite our best efforts to repair a friendship, sometimes it's best to let things go. But we become immobilized by our rumination, scared to follow through for fear of delaying the pain that awaits us on the other side.

Here are five signs a friendship no longer works:

1. *The only reason you're staying is because of how long you've been friends.* You think you owe it to history to keep going, and fear you'd have nothing to "show" for the time that you've invested if you let her go.
2. *There's a lack of trust.* No matter how you try to work around it, if you can't ever fully relax with her because you feel the need to be on guard (physically, mentally, emotionally), it's time to go. It's really simple: if you can't say "She has my back" with full confidence, you might need to reevaluate.
3. *Despite your best efforts, the friendship is not reciprocal.* While there will be seasons when things don't feel perfectly balanced, you

can't have a healthy friendship if one person starts to feel as if the relationship is sustained by her efforts alone.

4. *She doesn't value your feelings.* When you express frustration, disappointment, or sadness and your friend dismisses or minimizes your feelings, you may question whether she cares about you at all. As soon as you become skeptical about how much you matter to her, it might be time to terminate the relationship.

5. *You don't like who you are when you're together.* If the friendship only functions when you're operating inauthentically (e.g., complaining, people-pleasing, or performing more than usual), it's not a healthy dynamic.

It's so easy to recognize these signs in other friendships or when we're watching things play out between fictional characters on TV. But it's so difficult to recognize these breaking points in our own friendships. Once we do come to the realization that the expiration date is near, we have to take great care in the way that we release a woman we once had so much love for.

How to Let Go

As we continue to grow and evolve, seasons of friendship pruning are very common. But when we're in those moments of letting go, it can be tricky to figure out how to start the process.

One survey[66] of more than thirty-one thousand people found that, although two-thirds of Americans have ended a friendship, only 24 percent of people are *unsure* about whether they've ever been dumped by a friend. While it's not uncommon to terminate a friendship, there can be so much ambiguity in the way we choose to end things.

There are so many ways to let someone go, and we tend to choose our strategy according to a number of factors. Depending on the depth of the friendship, our conflict style, and the reason for the breakup, our method might include everything from a slow fade-out to a formal conversation.

I've noticed that the most common exit strategies can be categorized in four ways: the fade-out, the fake-out, the "flee-the-scene," and the formal bow. Let's look at the pros and cons of each.

Exit Strategy 1. The "Fade-Out"

Sometimes a friendship ends because both people decide it's just not a priority they want to maintain anymore. Maybe there was no egregious offense, no major betrayal to lament. You just don't have the energy to keep things going, and at some point, the demand of other obligations outweighs the duty you feel to the friendship.

When this happens, there's a silent agreement: Both women talk or text less and less until the friendship runs out of gas. You find a way to be perpetually "busy," with each person knowing she may never really circle back to the other. If someone asked them to point to a distinct moment in history when things began to shift, they probably couldn't tell you. But there was a mutual release on the grip they shared in their pursuit of each other.

This is the kind of ending most of us hope for. There's no intense blowup, no formal conversation—just a gradual, painless fade-out where no one is vilified and each escapes unscathed. If neither friend is desperate for closure and the decision to fade out is shared by both women, this might be a totally acceptable way to end things.

As long as both parties have accepted this fate, there's nothing to discuss.

But when one person wants out while the other wants to maintain status quo, a conversation is required to provide clarity and reconcile expectations.

Exit Strategy 2: The "Fake-Out"

Many of us get to a place where we're mentally committed to ending a friendship, but our actions tell a different story. We lean in to the contradictions hoping that somewhere in the midst of our inconsistencies, our friend will be the one to leave and we can be absolved of any "fault."

I was recently working with a woman named Charlotte who felt stuck in a ten-year friendship. The two had met in college, but the friendship had begun to feel burdensome. Charlotte told me her friend was always making backhanded compliments, criticizing her mothering, and engaging Charlotte in conversations that simply didn't interest her.

When I asked her why she continued to engage with the woman despite dreading every conversation, she acknowledged the messiness of it all.

"I hope that she gets the hint that I'm not interested, but then if we go for months without talking, I feel like I have to reach out. You know, to be polite."

These mixed signals reflected Charlotte's uncertainty about how to move forward, and they began to frustrate her friend, who felt confused by the whole thing. Despite Charlotte's desire to separate from the relationship, she continued to believe that things would end on their own. Somehow. Someday.

Some of us might find ourselves in the same space. With each passing day, we tell ourselves there's no urgency in terminating the friendship, another week wouldn't hurt. And in the meantime, we send mixed messages about our commitment and objective. Our own lack of clarity tends to trickle into the friendship, and we realize the dysfunction. But it just feels easier to take a passive role in the friendship's dissolution as we cross our fingers and hope for the best.

Whatever that might be.

Exit Strategy 3. "Fleeing the Scene"

Some of us choose to end a friendship by completely withdrawing without any kind of announcement or explanation. "Ghosting" is so abrupt and jarring that women say they've been genuinely traumatized by having friends disappear this way.

To be clear, we're not talking about those few exceptions. We're not talking about a friend who's committed an act so egregious that it's unsafe to continue the friendship. We're not talking about ending things with a friend who refuses to respect boundaries you've put up time and time again.

No.

We're talking about a *standard default setting* where you withdraw communication from people without letting them know why. When we "ghost" our friends, we center our comfort and rob them of the chance to say their piece or to have any kind of understanding or closure.

The whole thing can feel like an emotional assault.

I know I've been guilty of this.

At the time, I convinced myself I was doing it for noble reasons. I told myself that disappearing would be less hurtful than addressing the issue head on. *I don't want to hurt her feelings*, I'd tell others, justifying my inability to gather the courage to look her in the face and share my truth.

But I've also been on the receiving end. Being completely cut off without warning left me with the kind of pain that impacted my friendships for years to come.

It's not uncommon for me to hear from a woman who starts off talking about a current friendship issue and then somehow references being ghosted five, ten, even twenty years earlier. The impact makes her hypersensitive to doing anything wrong, careful not to repeat the misstep of crossing some invisible line. She struggles to accept love and validation of friends because she doesn't trust that they'll stick around. She second-guesses herself and holds in her true feelings and opinions, diligent about causing any discomfort that might push someone away.

When ghosting has this kind of impact, we have to be delicate in the way that we release our friends.

Ghosting may feel like the best option in the moment, but that's all it considers: the moment. Because it has bigger consequences long term, for both the "ghoster" and the one who's left behind.

Adopting this as a go-to method over time might reveal something about our lack of conflict resolution skills. It signals a need to reconsider the belief that an abrupt withdrawal of affection and communication would somehow be better than blindsiding the very women we claimed to care for at some point in our lives.

If we had a friendship of love and consideration, we must end the relationship with the same thoughtfulness and compassion we had during our time together.

If you decide to end the friendship in a way that may be interpreted as abrupt, that's your right. But communication makes all the difference. And regardless of whether others understand your reasons, you'll be free to move forward without guilt or shame or having caused undue harm when you decide you no longer want to invest in a friendship.

Exit Strategy 4. The "Formal Bow-Out"

As soon as your visions of the relationship's future are not in alignment, something has to happen to create a shared reality of the situation. If your friend wants to keep investing in the friendship but you want to pull away, depending on the circumstances, you might be obligated to have a conversation that puts both of you on the same page.

There's no doubt that she might be hurt and disappointed, but she'll also have the information she needs to recalibrate her efforts and find friends who are able to reciprocate and appreciate her in a way that you are no longer able to do.

Having a formal bow-out also allows you the space to move forward without the stress of trying to avoid her or the temptation to mislead her in any other way.

Now, the **way** you choose to have this conversation matters and depends largely on the context of your situation.

If you want to honor the integrity and history of your friendship, you'll want to talk as close to "in person" as you can get. This gives you a setting to communicate your sincerity with both words and nonverbal cues.

While it might feel easier to send a long text announcing your departure from the friendship (and then blocking her on socials), consider how much of your approach has been designed with the goal of avoiding discomfort.

Ending a friendship is inherently uncomfortable. Identify the parts of your strategy that would cause unnecessary feelings of confusion or disrespect.

Once you've determined the best way to deliver your message, you'll want to be careful about what you say. When you start speaking, try your best not to focus on all the ways that she's inadequate. Instead, highlight the ways you're going to pursue what you need.

For example, instead of, "You're just too negative and I can't deal with that kind of toxic energy," try "I think I need to be in spaces where I have a bit more freedom to be myself." Because ultimately, that's what this breakup is about. It's less about vilifying the person you're leaving, and more about you creating room in your life for friendships that are a better fit.

I also encourage you to be mindful about using too much "therapy-speak" in your explanation. I've noticed an increasing popularity in the use of phrases like "holding space," "limited capacity," and "respecting boundaries," and while this language is helpful for the person who is absolutely lost in how to begin articulating her desire for separation, it can feel cold and impersonal to the one on the receiving end.

You can't go from sharing secrets and holding her hair back in the bathroom to speaking to her like you're the head of HR. That kind of approach is simply incongruent to the context and history of your relationship, and while it feels "safer," the formality of it all can feel disrespectful.

Script out what you want to say and then reread your words, taking note of how many of these "therapy" phrases you've included. While they may certainly meet the objective of communicating your desire to end things, you have to ask yourself whether it feels appropriate to speak so formally with a friend you've known so intimately. Depending on the situation, this may be the best approach for ending things. But try to look for ways to allow yourself *to feel through* your message instead of protecting yourself with a sterile, professional language that doesn't reflect the nature of the relationship.

This might sound like:

"I've been thinking about our friendship a lot lately, and I'm not sure how I feel about it anymore. I don't know how we got to a place where there's so much tension, but if I'm being honest, I don't know how to move forward together.

"The last thing I want to do is hurt you because I care about you so much, but I also know that it's important for me to be in spaces where I feel comfortable being myself. I completely understand if you're upset with me or if you feel blindsided. Again, I don't want to hurt you. But I can't maintain this friendship anymore."

Yes, it will be awkward. Yes, she may get upset. And yes, you'll feel guilty for hurting someone that you care about. But at least she'll have to respect your directness and your honesty.

You'll also need to prepare for the possibility that your friend walks away with a narrative that mischaracterizes you as you're made out to be the "bad guy." Just because you plan your script and make the brave act of letting go doesn't mean you're guaranteed to be met with acceptance and understanding. It helps to remember that what you want most is to be in friendships that feel safe, offer ease, and make you feel like the best version of yourself.

And though she may not be able to appreciate it in the moment, letting go can be an act of generosity for you both.

How to Recover If It Happens to You

If someone in your life tells you that she doesn't want to be friends anymore, it can feel like a huge blow to your self-esteem, but there are a few things you can do to survive.

First, see whether your friend is open to giving you a reason for the breakup. She may be withholding back for the sake of protecting your feelings, but if you feel that you can handle it, let her know. This can be helpful in getting important data you need as you move forward on your friendship journey.

If she gives you a reason you don't agree with, try not to battle her—especially if it looks like her mind is made up on letting go. It can be really difficult to know that there's someone intent on misunderstanding who we are and what our intentions are, but it can be draining to try and change someone's mind if they're not open to listening and adapting their understanding.

Remember, you don't always have to agree with your friend's interpretation of things. But if she is not happy in the friendship, then from a place of love, find the strength to let her go.

If you don't have the opportunity to get closure, you'll have to create your own. I know—easier said than done. But consider your other options: bang her door down in the middle of the night demanding an explanation, interrogate mutual friends to see whether they have any intel, or ruminate incessantly about the endless possibilities of why she ended the friendship.

Each of these options leaves you empty-handed.

The best thing you can do is find a way to acknowledge the ambiguity of your situation, and say to yourself, "I don't know why things happened the way they did, and maybe I'll understand in the future. But today, I choose to be grateful for the lessons I learned in this friendship."

For most of us, our initial reaction to being dumped isn't, "Yes! I'm so lucky!" (Unless the entire friendship itself was a complete Dumpster fire, in which case, yes, you might find immediate relief.) It's hurtful, but identifying the parts of the friendship that we can be thankful for[67] is the first step to moving forward with less bitterness and resentment.

Choosing gratitude can help us become more resilient after suffering these kinds of losses. It helps us cope with the pain of this grief and loss. If you can force yourself to (a) identify something you appreciate about your time with your friend, and (b) think about ways your future friendships will benefit from what you learned in this one, you'll be better positioned to heal and move forward without bitterness or resentment.

The Art of Letting Go

After you tend to the tricky matters of reclaiming the clothes you loaned her, unsaving the Hulu password you shared (or not?), and determining which weeks you have "custody" of your mutual friends, you'll have to get to the business of moving on without her.

No matter how a friendship ends, moving on can be difficult for both people, but there are tangible things we can do to start the healing process.

Physically

Now is a great time to experiment with new routines and rituals, because depending on how integrated your friend was in your daily life, carrying on with the same things you did before might make her absence even more palpable.

Consider pursuing hobbies and interests that you put on hold while you were in that friendship. Switch up your weekly routines. Substitute any friendship rituals you had (e.g., Friday night happy hours) with other activities that not only distract you, but position you to invite new connections into your life.

Mentally

While it's tempting to rehash the details of your breakup (either in your head or with mutual friends), it can pose a major setback to your healing process. Worrying and reflecting are normal, but if you find your thoughts playing compulsively and consistently, it might be a sign[68] of harmful rumination.

Be careful to not fixate on things that don't have a solution, or constantly obsess over how things could be different. You'll want to get yourself to a place of acceptance as soon as you can, and this habit is often a major barrier.

Talking to others is helpful to process your feelings and receive validation, but you'll want to monitor when you're walking away from those interactions with clarity or confusion and anxiety. Grief is a messy, nonlinear process, so sometimes it might be a little of both. But be aware of how retelling the story is helping or hurting you.

Your social media habits can also mess with your peace of mind during this transition. Is it helpful to look at your friend's posts after you part ways? Are you searching for meaning and subtext in her captions and videos? What happens in your body when you watch her stories?

And when you post, are you doing so with the intention that she'll see it? Are you sharing content with her in mind in hopes of getting validation or subconsciously working to communicate that you're happy and thriving after the breakup? Evaluate the ways in which these habits lead to rumination, frustration, and confusion.

How to Grieve

There's no easy, fast-track way to move past a friendship breakup. It's one thing to know this intellectually, but it's another thing to experience it. Hold fast to the truth that it is a journey, and it'll prevent you from acting in impulsive ways that only cause unnecessary harm, confuse your mind, and delay your healing.

Kobe Campbell is a therapist and author of the book *Why Am I Like This?: How to Break Cycles, Heal Your Trauma, and Restore Your Faith.*[69] She often works with clients who are reeling after painful friendship breakups, and reminds them of the ways that grief can be complicated.

When I interviewed her about moving forward after a friendship ends, she illuminated me about ways to grieve the loss.

"Grief is the expression of deep sorrow. And the reason why I say 'expression' is because we are not grieving if we're not letting it out. Many of us are feeling the sadness, the anger, the confusion, but if we're not letting it out, we're not grieving.

"For many of us, we're not just grieving the loss of what we had in the past; we're letting go of the hopes we shared of the future. We may have expected to be in each other's weddings, raise each other's kids, and travel to different countries. When a friendship ends, we're forced to reconfigure our future."

Kobe suggests journaling ("because it can take the tangled threads and line them up to make them clear") and letting the person know how you feel—even if it's over.

"Whether they respond or not, you could say, 'Hey, this is how your behavior affected me. This is how it's made me feel.' That way this person knows how they affected you and, whether they decide to do something with it or not, they can't be confused about the consequences of their actions."

The Path to Forgiveness

The residual pain that we experience after a friendship breakup—specifically, the unforgiveness—is baggage we can sometimes journey with for so long that it becomes hard to imagine life without it.

The resentment we harbor from past relationships will inevitably shape relationships to come, because it's hard to fully engage in new friendships when you end each day pulling your grudges from under the pillow to cradle each night.

But this simply isn't the way.

So, how do we actually forgive?

First, understand that forgiveness is not a feeling; it's a decision. Once you make the conscious choice to let go, you may not experience immediate relief. It may take a while for your emotions to catch up. But taking your power back allows you to enjoy the fullness of all that your future friendships can offer.

To be able to fully release the resentment you have about your friend's betrayal (*forgiveness* in Greek literally means "to let go"), it helps to be clear on what forgiveness is *not*.

Forgiveness doesn't mean you want to reconcile and it doesn't mean you approve of the person's behavior. It also doesn't mean your friend won't be absolved of accountability. It just means that you have decided to no longer be tethered to her by carrying the bitterness as you move into new friendships. It means no longer storing mental mementos of the pain to revisit over and over again, keeping it just within reach in case you ever need it.

Releasing your resentment can be an act of self-care. And it might offer the freedom you need to invite new connections into your life.

When the End Makes You Feel Like a Failure

During a recent coaching session, my client told me how desperate she was to repair a dissolving friendship.

"I mean, I'm trying everything I can think of. I texted her to apologize and take ownership of my part in all of this. I dropped off a peace offering of her favorite cookies to her apartment. I emailed her to let her know I'm here when she's ready to talk. But she's still icing me out!"

Her volume rose as she recalled every attempt she'd made to resolve their tension.

"This friendship obviously means a lot you," I said. "Is that why you're putting so much effort into making this work?"

She seemed to look past me to somewhere in the distance as she admitted: "I just...can't have another friendship end. What would that say about me?"

One reason women struggle with friendship endings is the meaning they've assigned to it all. Many see the split as confirmation that they can't hold onto a successful friendship. Some wonder whether they're destined to fail forever. And some doubt themselves as a friend altogether.

In one survey about "friendship breakdowns" led by famous researcher Robin Dunbar, respondents reported an average of 1.5 breakdowns per person per year.[70] Women reported a slightly higher average than men, and since the same research found that we only have the cognitive capacity to maintain 150 social connections at a time, this works out to losing about 10 percent of our inner core each year.

Some friendships fade through no fault of our own. We move, change, and our priorities shift over time. Other friendships will end due to mistakes and misunderstandings, and all we can do is try to extract a meaningful lesson from the experience and move forward. But we must be careful of conflating friendship endings with markers of our inadequacy and incompetence.

It helps to remember that the ending of a friendship is not necessarily a failure.

And it doesn't mean that the friendship was a bad experience.

It just means that it's over.

Chapter 7 Questions

1. What do you think is the most difficult part about friendship breakups?
2. Think of a friendship that recently ended. Do you see the ending as a lack of compatibility or as a sign of your personal inadequacies?
3. If you're currently experiencing a friendship breakup, create a positive mantra to recite for the times when you feel overwhelmed by your grief.

Chapter 8 Preview Question

How have the lessons you've learned from former friendships shaped your current approach to friendship?

How to Make Friends Worth Fighting For

Despite her coldness, I still half-expected my neighbor Ariana to let me sit with her during lunch on my first day of high school. She was a junior and I was an incoming freshman, and I was hoping that she'd sense my terror and be welcoming to me just this once.

But when I walked into the cafeteria frantically searching for a familiar face, she whipped her head in the opposite direction so I didn't mistake her eye contact for an invitation.

I was anxious and embarrassed, with no one to sit next to during the most social time of the school day. So, I did what any terrified reject would do: I gripped my lunchbox, walked out of the cafeteria, and headed toward the bathroom to eat alone in my own private stall.

Fast-forward to senior year: I was the class president, playing on the basketball team, voted "Most Likely to Succeed," and attending the prom with one of the most handsome guys I knew. It was a total pivot from where I was on my first day of freshman year. Nibbling on that sad little sandwich in the bathroom three years prior, I couldn't have imagined how things would turn out.

I was on top of the world.

Until I left for college.

As a freshman at the University of Florida, I assumed that the confidence and friendships I'd collected in high school would transfer to college. But that didn't happen, and I once again found myself at the bottom of the food chain, friendless and insecure.

I had a small friend group (mostly guys) by sophomore year, but I eventually felt like they didn't "get" me, and those feelings of isolation put me in the market for new friends... again.

A few years after graduation, a close girlfriend and I began to drift apart, and it sent me on a search for women who could revive my hope in the love I'd just lost.

These transitions just kept happening: When I got my first job, had my first baby, moved to a new city, adopted new interests—each transitional season came with the same question: *How do I make new friends?*

As a friendship coach, this is the number one question that I hear. And typically, it comes with some kind of qualifier:

How do I make new friends *as a mom?*
How do I make friends *in a new city?*
How do I make friends *after a divorce?*
How do I make friends *when I have social anxiety?*

I hope this shows us that we will always be having to make new friends. So, it helps to develop the skill to invite new connections into our lives... and the skill of *deepening* those friendships once we've got them.

Finding Your People

When we were in school, it was much easier to make friends. Sure, we dealt with a fear of rejection, an underdeveloped sense of self, and limited resources, but it felt like there was no shortage of opportunities.

Research[71] suggests our social networks continue to expand until about the age of twenty-six, at which point they begin to shrink exponentially. This is likely because, up until this point, we're all in the same life season and on the same trajectory. But once we hit our midtwenties, those friendships begin to splinter as we each prioritize different things—career advancement, establishing family ties, developing new interests and adjusting our lifestyles.

Then suddenly, we find that, for the first time, we have to facilitate friendships on our own, without the backdrop of a social institution to tell us what to do, where to go, who to sit next to.

So, let's look at six strategies that you can use to help you begin creating new friendships as an adult.

Strategy 1. Go with who you know.

Many of us have people in our network we've dismissed as potential friends for whatever reason—too young, too loud, too weird, not weird *enough*—but this is a good place to begin creating new friendships.

Some of the best friendship stories you'll hear are people who say, "She started out as my hairdresser/coworker/favorite barista, and then we both thought, 'We should be friends!'" Are you overlooking people you know because you always thought that "making friends" has to start from scratch?

Think about an acquaintance you have who you've never entertained as a potential friend. The next time you talk to her, introduce a topic that you two normally don't discuss. If you have a coworker who you only talk business with, make a joke about how little you know about her and ask what she does for fun. The next time you talk to your boyfriend's cousin who you may normally keep at arm's length, ask, "So, what are you watching these days?"

Multiplexity is the concept of having relationships with people who play multiple roles in your life (e.g., your coworker and your friend), and research shows that these friendships can be especially enriching.[72] So, get curious about the people you already know and allow yourself to be surprised by the potential.

Strategy 2. Connect with a "concierge."

Hotel concierges tend to be very "plugged in," using their knowledge of the local area to help guests maximize their experience.

Many of us know a woman who functions this way—she thrives on making introductions between people, seems to have ties to people from different walks of life, and remains perpetually active on the scene with an expansive social network. Leverage this person's intel to help you make connections with entirely new networks.

Once you identify your "social concierge" (it can be an acquaintance or coworker), reach out to her with a text or direct message with something like:

Hey! I'm trying to be more intentional about getting plugged in and I thought of you. It seems like you're pretty "in the know," and so I thought I'd ask: Are there any places or events around town that you think are worth checking out?

Framing your request this way is productive for a few reasons:

So many of us want to make new friends, but we're afraid to make our desire known for fear that we'll look desperate or clingy. Reaching out to express a need gets you one step closer getting your need met.

This phrasing is also effective because research shows that when we tell people why we specifically selected them for the job, they're more likely to help. Telling your "concierge" why she's the perfect person for you to ask demonstrates a certain level of thoughtfulness that might make her even more responsive.

The right woman will be flattered that you see her as a well-connected person, and she'll likely be happy to help. If she seems reluctant (or if she doesn't respond altogether), remember that even a no is helpful data because it informs you of where to invest your energy. Turn, instead, to someone else with a willingness to help. And then, don't feel ashamed about communicating your needs.

Strategy 3. Become a "regular."

Establishing a routine isn't necessarily sexy or revolutionary, but it can be incredibly helpful when trying to create new friendships. Consistency breeds familiarity, and familiarity is a helpful primer in talking to someone you don't know.

Think about something you can do each day (or week) with consistency. Can you walk your dog at the same time every day? Can you commit to going to a yoga class consistently for the same two days each week? Can you attend the monthly trivia night at the cute local bar? Can you finally volunteer for a cause you're passionate about? If you work from home, can you commit to working from your favorite coffee shop every Friday morning?

Since people are creatures of habit, it's likely that you'll see the same faces congregating and passing by. Seeing those same faces makes it easier to say hello and begin building rapport, because it's less intimidating to approach someone when you've locked eyes a few times and have exchanged a few "heys," and these people become "familiar strangers."

Note: I know that women must be especially cautious about having public routines that others can monitor and abuse. Always consider safe ways to integrate these concepts to fit your lifestyle and comfort level.

Strategy 4. Leverage technology.

It's become increasingly normal to make friends online. What used to be thought of as a last resort is now a go-to strategy for women who want to be strategic about meeting other people.

Last year, Bumble—one of the world's largest dating apps—asked me to be its resident friendship expert as it launched its new app, Bumble For Friends. It turns out that so many people were visiting the dating app to find friends that they developed this app for people in a season of intentionally pursuing platonic connections.

When I secured the partnership, I was suddenly flooded with stories from members who were eager to share their story with me. One story was from a friend trio—Natalie, Kaycee, and Nainee—who met on the app, became best friends, attended each other's weddings, and even got matching tattoos. They credit technology to their friendship love story.

Using technology to help you meet like-minded women isn't desperate; it's resourceful. This is especially true if you have children, work unconventional hours, or travel a lot.

To make the most of your virtual "friending" experience, there are a few **things you'll want to avoid**:

1. *Using negative language.* When building your profile, you'll want to focus on what you *are* looking for instead of what you dislike. So, you wouldn't write "I don't click with people who..."; you'd say, "I tend to get along with people who...." Positive-framing might help others more quickly determine whether they'd be a good match.

2. *Skipping sections.* Maximize the real estate on your profile by answering all of the prompts because this shows your range and personality. Not only do algorithms favor profiles that are more complete, but you'll also signal your effort and intention by taking the time to respond to everything (as opposed to skipping sections and risk seeming uninterested, lazy, or noncommittal).

3. *Listing generic interests.* When there are so many people dancing in the digital town square, you have to stand out. Instead of listing "music, travel, and food" as your interests, get specific. What's an album you can listen to without skipping a single song? What's the story behind the best meal you ever had? Which travel spot makes you feel most like yourself and why? These questions still speak to your love for music, travel, and food, but they work to show your sense of humor, values, and personality.

After you connect with a woman you like, humanize your virtual exchanges with videos or voice notes and then work to take things in person (as long as you feel comfortable). This is the key to keeping momentum and seeing whether your chemistry online translates to the real world.

Strategy 5. Try "bookending" your next event.

Sometimes, in our effort to skip the awkwardness of small talk, we intentionally arrive late (and leave early) when attending events. But the moments immediately before and after an event offer an opportunity to actually engage with other attendees to build the rapport you'd need to establish and grow a friendship.

At the next gathering you attend, arrive early to get the lay of the land, help set up, or bump into others who are getting settled in. These are opportunities you won't have once the event begins and the environment is no longer conducive to undistracted conversation.

And then once the event is over, you'll want to grab your purse and head straight for the exit, determined to get home and settle into that Netflix binge (introvert!) or head to the next gathering (extrovert!). But I challenge you to hang around for the length of a song. That's it. Just one song. During that time you can *slowly* pack up your space, go up to the event coordinator (or teacher, facilitator) and tell them how much you enjoyed yourself, take a look at the art on the walls, and pour yourself one more cup of water for the road.

Be aware of how approachable you are while you navigate the space. Be conscious about scrolling on your phone while you're walking around ("I'm engrossed in a very important task; please don't interrupt."); not making casual eye contact with people as they pass by ("I don't want to connect with anyone right now"), walking too quickly ("I have somewhere to be—don't slow me down!"), or wearing a serious expression ("I'm not happy; approach at your own risk."). I'm certainly not suggesting you walk around smiling like a psychopath, but you do need to be aware of how others may experience your presence. Does it invite or does it unknowingly make people rule you out as a receptive connection?

Last year, I was working with a beautiful woman named Leyla who owned her own business, regularly attended the gym, and frequently participated in various networking events. She had no problem initiating conversations, but she was convinced that she was missing opportunities to engage others because she was so on the go.

She tried the "bookend" strategy at an aerobics class to help her slow down and be more present, so she applied it the following week when she attended her aerobics class. As soon as the teacher dismissed everyone, Leyla lingered and packed her equipment slowly. She also made casual eye contact and smiled with other women as they exited. While she was packing, three women approached her and commented on how rigorous the class was and began to ask her about herself. Within minutes, they were exchanging social media information, taking pictures together (!) and arranging to meet for coffee.

Leyla positioned herself for connection by slowing down, intentionally scanning the room, and projecting a warmth that attracted others—an opportunity she'd been missing each week when she put her head down and raced out the door.

Strategy 6. Take yourself out on more dates.

From a practical standpoint, if you say you want to meet friends who love to rock climb, read, and ride horses, then where will those women be? At the climbing gym, in the bookstore aisles, and in the horse stables. Occupy the spaces that bring you joy if you want to create moments of serendipity with like-minded people.

Besides, there's nothing more attractive than seeing a woman in her element, enjoying herself.

Here's how it's done:

On your solo dates, be sure to occupy the most high-traffic spaces.

If you go to a restaurant, don't sit alone and read a book (unless you want to!). Try to sit in a relatively active area (such as the bar) doing things that invite conversation. If you go to a social event, be mindful of the spaces where people are coming and going, such as near the bathroom hall, the drinks, or the food where others naturally congregate.

Then, strike up a conversation with someone nearby. Try offering a compliment (works every time), asking a question about how they know the host, or commenting on the food or the music.

Because friendship begins with rapport, and rapport begins with "hello."

A Note About Rejection

I know the fear of rejection has the power to immobilize us, preventing us from pursuing connection with others. We don't want people to withdraw from our advances, sending us spiraling as we deal with hurt and embarrassment.

But here's one reframe that will help.

At the risk of sounding "life coach-y," you have to view connection as who you are, not something you do. People who embrace connection as a part of their identity are going to pursue others because it's who they are. But if you see "going first" as something you do only if you get some kind guarantee that you'll be accepted, then you become a reactive player on your friend-making journey.

If a stranger is wearing a beautiful scarf, say so. If a friend you haven't spoken to in a year crosses your mind, send her a text. If there's a new brunch spot you've been dying to try, think of who good company would be and extend an invitation.

Research[73] tells us that we tend to greatly underestimate how much people appreciate us reaching out, so lean in to those nudges. You might be surprised by how many people are relieved that you had the courage to go first (a skill that you need to not only start a friendship, but to sustain it).

As Nicholas Epley wrote in his book *Mindwise*,[74] "Nobody waves, but almost everybody waves back."

Friendship on a Continuum

Once you've used these strategies to bring new social connections into your life, you'll begin to engage them in an attempt to create genuine friendships.

But to manage expectations and experience more satisfaction on your friend-making journey, there are a few things we must understand about the levels of friendship.

First, try thinking of relationships as a continuum. On the far left, we have relationships with "no connection." On the far right, we have what Carole Robin—coauthor of the book *Connect: Building Exceptional Relationships with Family, Friends, and Colleagues*[75]—refers to as "exceptional relationships." And not every relationship will make it to that level.

"Along the [continuum], there's just plain old 'robust,' and 'functional,' and 'satisfying.' Once you learn how to move a relationship to that, *then* you can decide if you want to take a few of them farther."

Not only is there a scale for us to conceptualize ways to create depth with our connections, but we also have certain limitations around the number of close relationships we can maintain at one time.

Anthropologist and evolutionary psychologist Robin Dunbar[76] has found that our brain can only cognitively handle a certain number of connections (150, to be exact), and because of the time and energy required to invest in superclose friendships, not every connection can fit into the "inner circle."

His research finds that there's cognitive space for three to five superclose relationships, ten to fifteen solid relationships, and then the numbers continue to increase as the degree of connection decreases.

We need our close relationships so that we can experience platonic intimacy. But we also need those people in our outer circles (referred to as "weak ties") because they, too, add value to our lives. Research[77] shows that these relationships boost our mood, make us empathetic, and connect us to new social groups. (And people who have more "weak ties" tend to be happier than those who don't.) But it's in our close relationships where we find the platonic intimacy we crave. They stabilize, challenge, and affirm us.

Once you have people in your life whose company you enjoy well enough and some of those connections blossom into friendship, consider the different things they offer instead of focusing on what they don't. It's nice to have a singular bestie who checks every box, but the search for a ride-or-die might block you from enjoying an even more robust friendship landscape.

In her book *The Life Council*,[78] Laura Tremaine shares the concept of having multiple friends and recognizing them for the unique role they each play in your life. She suggests different friend types, such as the "daily duty friend" (someone who's in the details of life with you each day), the "mentor" (the one who offers guidance), and the "fellow obsessive" (a woman with whom you share common interests).

While some friendships may check every box, we might experience more abundance in our lives if we recognize that we can get everything we need from a collective instead of expecting it to all come from one single individual.

Clinging to this truth will help you enter your friendship journey with more of an abundance mind-set, understanding that the people you meet may not all move up to the "exceptional" side of the friendship continuum, but that they may sit somewhere along the line that still offers value in some unique way.

Once you find those connections and they show promise of something more, you might become intentional about cultivating a richer relationship. But how do you turn acquaintances into something more?

How to Find Resilient Friendships

Resilient friendship involves a dynamic where those involved respond to challenges together in a healthy, positive way. While we benefit from having friendships in various places on the continuum, the satisfaction we get from deeper friendships is superimportant.

The process of forming close friendships tends to bring a lot of our personal issues and complexities to the surface. When people refer to the "work" that friendship requires, it's about so much more than the external effort we have to make to keep the relationship going. There's a lot that we have to reconcile internally to enjoy healthy relationships.

Here are four beliefs we need to adopt to enjoy the fullness of what resilient friendships offer:

1. Friendships don't just happen.

If you think that friendships should unfold without much effort, you might be setting yourself up for disappointment in the long run.

In one study,[79] researchers asked participants whether they believed that making friends should be easy and natural, or expected that it would require work. They followed up with the participants five years later and discovered that those who said that friendship should be easy were reporting greater feelings of loneliness than those who said they believe it takes work.

If you expect your friendships to happen without much intention or investment, that belief influences your behavior. "Low-maintenance friendships" have been a hot topic for the last few years as people express a desire for the kind of relationship that doesn't require much from them. And while we certainly don't want to feel drained by or obligated to others, the satisfaction we derive from these friendships is sometimes correlated to how much we put in.

Remembering special dates, sending check-in texts, coordinating dates to see or talk to each other, pushing past our fears to show up more vulnerably, occasionally allowing ourselves to be inconvenienced to tend to their needs—it's the kind of effort that is known to have a high emotional and relational return.

If most of your friendships feel active and connected but you can say they're effortless, then get curious about whether that means your friends are the ones doing the heavy lifting to keep momentum in the relationship!

2. Trust takes time.

Sometimes, you meet a woman you just vibe with and while it doesn't make sense to others, you feel like you've known this woman all your life. Becoming "fast friends" can be exciting, but this quick intensity speaks to *chemistry*, not friendship.

In fact, there's research that finds that it takes thirty-four hours[80] to take someone from an acquaintance to a friend. While chemistry can certainly lead to a wonderful friendship, it takes time for others to show you their character and for you to demonstrate your trustworthiness to one another.

In our hunger for connection, we may try to expedite the process, manufacturing a sense of closeness to skip past the get-to-know you stage. But in getting to know one another, we learn our needs, desires, and boundaries. We're also able to face small "micro-tensions" with one another, revealing our capacity for forgiveness, acceptance, and resilience.

3. Knowing your attachment style can inform the decisions you make.

Attachment theory is all about how we bond with others, and our "style" is shaped by both our relationship with our caregivers as children *and* our present relationships. The most common types are secure, anxious, and avoidant.

I learned a lot about this after reading Dr. Marisa G. Franco's book *Platonic: How the Science of Attachment Can Help You Make—and Keep—Friends*,[81] and it helped me better understand patterns when clients share their friendship history with me.

The goal is to work toward becoming securely attached. Dr. Franco summarizes this belief: "I am worthy of love, and I trust other people to give me that love."

Securely attached people have a strong sense of self-worth and have a generally trusting attitude toward others. Anxious people may behave in a "clingy" way because they fear being rejected, bending to please others even to their own detriment. Avoidant people end to avoid intimacy and prefer their independence (also driven by a fear of rejection).

Dr. Franco explains that our attachment style is often exposed when we project certain assumptions on moments of ambiguity.

Let's look at an example to see this in action.

A newish friend hasn't texted you back in a few days. Her delay could be due to myriad reasons. The assumptions you make in these ambiguous spaces aren't only shaped by your attachment style, but they dictate your behavior.

Secure attachment: "Maybe she's busy. I'm sure we'll reconnect when the time's right."

Anxious attachment: "Maybe she's mad at me. Maybe she lost interest in me. I'm going to message her a few more times—maybe even drive by her house!—to make sure we're okay."

Avoidant attachment: "It's no big deal if she doesn't text me back. I prefer my own company anyway."

Sometimes, during coaching sessions, a client reveals her attachment style in the way that she speaks about her friendships.

Secure clients have said things like:

- "I guess I'm a little scared to put myself out there, but I'm going to try."
- "I definitely try to support my friends when they need it, and I'm trying to get more comfortable asking for support when I need it, too."
- "I'm going to have a hard talk with my friend this weekend. It'll be awkward, but I know she loves me and would want to work through this together."
- "I think I have to let this friendship go because it doesn't feel healthy."

Anxious clients have said things like:

- "I'm not going to tell her how I feel because I know she'll blow up and stop talking to me."
- "I guess I have a tendency to overshare in new friendships. But that helps make us closer faster."
- "I think they have another group chat that I'm not in. They're probably talking about me."

- "Now that she's married, it's like she has no time for me. I knew this would happen. I don't know if she even likes me anymore."

Avoidant clients have said things like:

- "I only give people one chance. As soon as you let me down, I'm done."
- "No, I'd rather just deal with it myself. I'm not going to cry to her about how I feel."
- "I'm not going to compromise on my expectations. But, these days, there just aren't many people who even know how to be a friend."
- "I don't need to hang with my friends all the time. I can go months without talking to her and that's just fine with me."

I encourage you to spend some time learning about attachment styles to understand why you show up the way you do in your friendships. Because if you continue to enter into relationships where you *consistently* feel that you aren't heard or where you don't experience true closeness and connection, you might be able to trace it back to this.

The good news is that it's possible to cultivate a more secure attachment style, and once you do, you'll experience the kind of healthy friendships you've been looking for.

4. Believe that you have something to offer.

If you don't believe you have anything worthy to offer in a friendship, that belief is going to manifest itself in ways that cripple your potential for depth in your friendships.

If you think you're "too much," you'll downplay your needs and desires so that you don't overwhelm others. If you think you're not interesting, you'll personalize your friends' innocuous words and behavior as see it as "confirmation" that they're getting bored with you or that you'll soon be forgotten.

If you don't think people would like the real you, friendship will always be a performance as you work to compensate for the traits that you believe to be repellant. Or worse, you'll attract friends who mistreat you.

Self-verification theory is a psychological concept that suggests that people gravitate toward those who see (and treat) them in a way that's consistent with how they see themselves—even if that view is negative.[82] This means that women who don't see themselves in a positive light may subconsciously attract friends who see them the same way!

Get really clear about your worth and find a way to believe that you have something to offer this world because it influences what you accept and how you engage. You'll likely initiate more, speak honestly during conflict, and show up more authentically in your platonic relationships as you balance a strong sense of self with an ability to connect with others.

Identifying Your Friendship Values

When we're in a friends-making season, it's common to hear people say, "I'm looking for my people." This conjures romanticized ideas of hanging out with people who just "get us" and those ideas fuel our hunt for platonic soulmates.

It's as if we believe that we'll have the experience we're looking for if we can only find these people who are predestined to be our girls. It's as if these "ready-made" friends are out there walking around somewhere on this floating rock, and having the friendship of our dreams is only a matter of "finding them."

But that mind-set could be detrimental to creating long-lasting, resilient friendships.

When you prioritize finding the right "people," you (unintentionally!) adopt a critic's mind-set. Everyone you meet is subject to being measured against your idea of what the ideal friend would be like, and research suggests that adopting this mind-set may make you less willing to work through challenges[83] with a friend, because you'll see conflict as a sign that the friendship isn't meant to be.

To build resilient friendships, focus less on finding the right individuals and think instead about the values you want in your platonic relationships overall.

Make a list of what you want to experience in these new friendships, then look for the ways each new connection reflects these values back to you. This exercise will help you connect with people who embody these values, as well as determine how *you* would be required to show up.

Here is an example:

Friendship Value	How I show up	What I look for in others
Consistency	I will do my best to follow through with plans that I make with friends.	An effort to keep their word
Open-mindedness	I'll be mindful of how quickly I rush to judgment when friends share things with me.	A spirit of curiosity
Accountability	I'll listen humbly when friends call me out, instead of blaming or getting defensive.	A safe space for me to lovingly challenge them
Positivity	I will be mindful of the energy I bring to my friends.	Help to see the world through a more hopeful and optimistic lens

How to Deepen Your Friendships with the "A.D.O.R.E." Practice

So many of us would say that we have no problem connecting with new people, but we struggle to turn our acquaintances into actual friends. I don't know about you, but whenever I hear people talk about pouring into their friendships, it so often feels like a random list of "nice" things to do: *Surprise her with a cup of coffee! Send her a "just thinking of you" text.*

Yes, these are obviously sweet gestures, but investing in friendship is about so much more than random acts of kindness. In fact, it's not random at all—it's intentional. If there's a woman in your life who you'd like to grow with, you'll have to make thoughtful efforts to move in a particular direction with her over time.

I created the A.D.O.R.E. Practice to make it easy to help you know what to do to deepen your relationships with other women. Not only will you experience more connection, but it buffers the relationship against the strain of inevitable conflict.

This practice includes five concepts that—when working together—make your friends feel increasingly seen, valued, and supported over time.

Appreciation

To appreciate your friend means finding ways to demonstrate that you recognize her full value.

Research[84] finds that expressing gratitude creates more positive regard between you and another person and *verbalizing* that gratitude has more of an impact than simply feeling appreciative. It's tempting to assume that our friends know we appreciate them and that the knowledge alone should be enough. But we have to look for ways to make our feelings tactical.

Expressing your appreciation not only helps your friend feel truly seen, but it has the power to dilute future friction. We're better able to take hard feedback and assume positive intentions with someone who's laid the groundwork of affirmation and care.

To lean in to this practice, you don't have to necessarily use the word "appreciate." Just think of ways you can verbalize knowledge of her worth.

The day after a hangout, reach out with a reflection:

I'm still thinking about that joke you made last night. Seriously, thank you for being our resident comedian.

You can also tell her the impact of something tangible she's done for you:

Hey, thank you for your consistent check-ins. This has been a really hard season, but talking to you has given me so much perspective.

You should also communicate an appreciation for who she is outside of what she can do for you specifically:

I admire the way you stand up for yourself or *You're so good at your job. Seriously, they're lucky to have you.*

Desire

Expressing desire shouldn't be reserved for our romantic relationships. We all want to be wanted, worthy of pursuit.

When a friend expresses a desire to know you or spend time with you, it gives you permission to do the same. When two friends feel safe enough to freely pursue each other, it increases the transparency and momentum in the relationship.

Desire makes our friends feel special and it also shows them that they're worth fighting for during times of conflict.

There are a few different ways to show an active interest and pursuit in your friendships.

- Make plans without being prompted. (This says, *I desire to spend time with you.*)
- Tell her you missed her company at an event she didn't come to. (This says, *I desire your companionship.*)
- Ask her questions about her childhood, current interests, and various life developments. (This says, *I desire to get to know you better.*)

It can feel vulnerable to openly express a desire for someone. We fear it'll make us clingy or weak—too invested. But the right people will see it as endearing, authentic, and honest, and they'll be glad to have someone who's unafraid to pursue her friends with intention.

Openness

The "Beautiful Mess Effect" refers to our inclination to like people more after they've been vulnerable with us. We resonate with those who can show us the fullness of their humanity.

For women, we fear being vulnerable in four ways. We fear being rejected for looking weak (*What if I look too sensitive?*), weird (*What if this makes me different from everyone else?*), wrong (*What if I look foolish?*), and wonderful (*What if they think I'm shining too brightly?*).

The key is to create a space where it's safe to take these kinds of risks. Your friends should know that it's okay to be open because you'll do your best to make sure they don't feel judged, attacked, or misunderstood.

Openness in the beginning stages of friendship-building also sets the foundation for people to navigate conflict without the use of defense mechanisms down the road, and that kind of authenticity is key in resilient friendships.

Practice vulnerability by sharing things about your life, trying something new in front of her, allowing yourself to receive help, and telling her that you like her!

Building a culture of openness also involves being mindful of the things you don't do. Be mindful of how you respond when your friends are vulnerable with you. Do you show a visible discomfort? Do you criticize? Do you "poke fun" in a way that could make them shut down? Think about ways you can make your friendship feel safe enough for each of you to freely share your opinions, make mistakes, and challenge each other.

Reliability

We know that trust is important in a friendship, but we have to consistently show our friends that they can count on us through keeping our word and following through with commitments.

Demonstrating reliability can buffer any uncertainty or skepticism that may begin to grow within us when we're experiencing everything from a momentary disagreement to a long season of tension. When you know that someone's dependable, it makes you respect her and keep the faith during times of conflict.

You can show your friend that you're trustworthy by doing things that prove she can count on you.

Avoid the temptation to cancel plans. While she might tell you it's no big deal, it trains her not to take you seriously when you make commitments.

You can also try remembering little things she's shared with you about her personal interests and follow up unprompted with helpful resources or links to things that show you were attentive.

You also want to be mindful of habits that can make you seem undependable. If you gossip about other friends or share others' personal secrets, she can't help but make a mental note of how you don't honor people's confidences.

Trust is the bedrock of any close relationship, so we must be careful of the things we say and do that would make her question whether we have her back.

Experiences

When we share experiences with our friends, it not only attaches deeper meaning to the experience itself, but we associate those positive feelings with the person we shared the experience with.

Look for ways to enjoy each other in different settings and contexts to create that will bond you.

Start by asking her to join you on the things you normally do alone (cooking, Netflix, hiking).

Cooking, watching a new show, hiking—you can do each of these things in isolation. But research has revealed something known as the "amplification effect," which states that whatever we feel during an experience tends to be magnified when we're sharing it with someone else.

You can also try meeting your friends in *their* happy places. Does your friend light up when she's skating, or at the dog park, or crocheting? How can you join her in the spaces that light her up? And how could these experiences deepen her appreciation for you?

The key to forming safe and supportive friendships is to be intentional about our approach. These kinds of healthy friendships develop when we're committed to showing up authentically, extending grace, and making deliberate moves toward deep connections.

Chapter 8 Questions

1. How have your expectations of friendship changed over the last five years?
2. Which aspect of the friend-making journey comes more easily to you: making friends or deepening friendships?
3. Which aspect of the A.D.O.R.E. Practice feels most vulnerable for you? Which one do you wish you received more from others?

Chapter 9 Preview Question

Can you recall a time when receiving platonic love from another woman healed something inside of you? If not, what kinds of gestures of love have you been craving?

Chapter 9

Loving You, Loving Me

Standing at the head of the table, I scanned each face in the room and felt my eyes begin to sting.

Staring back at me were ten women I'd invited to a private dinner at one of the most beautiful event venues in Tampa. I was two months postpartum and had squeezed into a skirt I rented from a shop downtown, wanting to look my best.

A few weeks before, I sent emails to each woman at the table, telling her how much I appreciated her, and I included an invitation to join me for an intimate Valentine's dinner. When they arrived, I gave them roses and surprised them with a serenade from a local musician who dazzled them with a Jill Scott song. I looked on as they got choked up, unsure of how to receive a platonic gesture offered with such…romance.

I was painfully aware of how sentimental—how cheesy—it all seemed. Maybe it was the hormones from pregnancy. Maybe it was a new compulsion to express platonic desire. But after years of withholding the fullness of my love from friends, I was ready to pour it out without embarrassment or apology.

When you spend hours a week studying the research on women's conflict and connection, you can't help but have your own relationships shaped by what you learn. And since doing this work, I've realized that the reason I spent so much time holding back in my friendships is because I didn't totally love myself.

How could I share the parts of me that I hadn't yet come to accept?

With guy friends, it felt easy to conceal my awkwardness and weaknesses. *They don't know what to look for,* I'd think. *They're so easy to distract.* But when I look into a woman's eyes, I know that I can't fool her. She sees me for real. And I felt exposed.

Before, the idea of being seen by other women made me fearful. I was afraid that they'd see the parts of me that were ugly, unintelligent, and uncertain. I didn't feel feminine or friendly enough. I wasn't as stylish or sexy.

But as soon as I grew more comfortable with who I am as a woman, I began to see other women as an extension of myself. It became difficult to shrink in front of them. It felt unnatural to try to differentiate myself with claims like "I'm not like other girls." I embraced the fact that, in so many ways, I'm *just* like other girls, and that brings me comfort.

But standing among friends at my Valentine's dinner, I felt emboldened. That evening marked the beginning of a new chapter. I was giving myself permission to freely express platonic desire.

And it was only possible because, bit by bit, love from other women has helped me love myself.

It happens all the time.

It happened the day I allowed a new friend to see me bare-faced for the first time. Embarrassed by my secret moles and blemishes, I felt naked. But she gently cupped my face and showed me new ways to apply my makeup—something I still struggled with as a thirty-five-year-old woman.

It happened when my friends noticed how overwhelmed I'd become while hosting my four-year-old's birthday party. My hyperindependence wouldn't allow me to ask for help, so as soon as they saw me drowning, they jumped into action without saying a word.

It happened after making a life-altering decision in a sterile clinic when I was twenty-three. As depression crept in, a friend sat with me all night, bringing me Tylenol and heating pads.

It happened when a friend sat and listened patiently as I cried over a man I couldn't let go of despite his repeated unfaithfulness. She poured wine and typed a list of all the reasons he was "the worst," and she showed it to me every time I considered dating him again to remind me of my worth.

It happened when I made a snarky joke with a coworker I wanted to befriend, and she slapped her legs while laughing heartily and saying, "Wow, you're funny." It gave me permission to believe I might be funny. All because she said so.

It happened after I had my first baby, and the mommy group I'd initially dismissed as "weird" rallied around me and showed me how to breastfeed my son.

It happened when I was sitting on the couch with my mother and she shared random memories of her late friend Miranda, offering a picture of the kind of friendships I desire for myself.

And it keeps on happening.

Now as I give myself permission to love them back, I've formed friendships that are so worth the fight.

And not just the little fights we have between us . . . but the fight within me to love myself.

Acknowledgments

First, I want to thank Jesus for being the ultimate model of friendship. Thank you for modeling how to forgive, love our neighbors, and speak truth in love. Thank you for the opportunity to do this work. Help me to be a light.

To the literary team that made this possible, thank you for seeing the vision and helping me bring this to life. Kim, you've been such a blessing in my life, calming my fears and offering guidance during the times I was discouraged. Thank you for your confidence and encouragement—you're an incredible agent and I appreciate you so much.

Renée, you have been such a light. Thank you for your notes and direction, and for the energy you brought to this experience. Nzinga, Hachette, and the Stonesong team: thank you for believing in this project—it wouldn't exist without your commitment to the vision.

To the Friend Forward community—look at us, y'all! We made it.

In addition to my book team and community, *Fighting for Our Friendships* also exists because of the strength, support, knowledge, and loving correction I've received from various women on my personal friendship journey.

Mom, thank you for being my first example of what it means to be a friend. Your guidance and tough love showed me what it means to be a woman who supports other women. I love you.

Quanna—I've said this before but I'll say it again: I know the world would be a better place if every woman had a "Quanna" of her own. To me, you are the standard for friendship, and my heart swells when I think of how much value you add to my life. I look at the way you carry yourself—with a little bit of Trina, a little bit of T.D. Jakes—and I count myself lucky to be friends with one of the coolest women I know.

Jaime Corinna—I've got your back. Always. Thank you for helping me bring this to life, and thank you for more than ten years (!!!) of friendship.

Katy & Marissa & Crystina—You are proof that people should reject the whole idea of "no new friends." Thank you for the gift of laughter. Our growing friendship has been so exciting, and I'm looking forward to all the adventures ahead.

Chauvon—Thank you for being such an encourager and a light. I'm grateful for our "boomerang" friendship.

Yamel and the entire Belen family—Thank you for your check-ins and support in watching baby Harper during the early stages of the book-writing process. I appreciate you!

Kynesha, Karissa, Sonny, Gabby, Sarasota Crew + Kavita, Cousin Sam, Kelly, Auntie Carol, my book club ladies and mommy groups—Thank you for being women who model different versions of who I'd like to be, as a mother and a friend and a Christian and a wife.

Sam Lee! Thank you for keeping me organized for the past three years and making sense of every scattered voice note. You've watched the business grow, and I wouldn't be able to enjoy these opportunities without having someone like you running the show behind the scenes. Malorie, thank you for your insightful edits. To my author support group and "Connection Matters" WhatsApp group: You all have taught me so much and I am honored to work alongside you in this industry. I admire each of you so much.

Thank you to the Bumble team for the opportunity of a lifetime, and for your commitment to helping people around the world create new friendship stories.

To my baby girl, Harper: Whenever I get discouraged, I think of your little face. Seeing mama work late is all you've ever known. When this book deal happened, you were in my belly. By the time it's out in the world, you'll be 2.5 years old. What a long journey! I love you, and I look forward to all the friendships that await you in this world.

And to the special boys in my life: Dad, you are always my number one fan. Thank you for hyping me up. Elijah, my first born: Thank you for sharing Mama for the past four years. Everything I do is for you and baby Harper. You bring so much joy to my life. Keith: Thanks for playing Barbies with me when we were little and none of my friends were able to come out and play.

And finally, to my husband, Ryan: I love you so much. You've been here from day one, encouraging me through every setback, helping me form new ideas, and—while you are definitely not my target demo—you've spent countless hours serving as an unofficial focus group. Thank you for being my rock. I am forever grateful for your intelligence, protection, and understanding. As I learned more about what the research has to say about friendship, I realized that friendship is at the heart of romantic relationships, and I hope that through it all, we'll always be friends first.

Notes

1. "Interconnecting," Google search, May 15, 2023, www.google.com.

2. Liz Mineo, "Good Genes Are Nice, but Joy Is Better," *Harvard Gazette*, April 11, 2017, https://news.harvard.edu/gazette/story/2017/04/over-nearly-80-years-harvard-study -has-been-showing-how-to-live-a-healthy-and-happy-life/.

3. Robert Waldinger and Marc Schulz, *The Good Life* (New York: Simon and Schuster, 2023).

4. Shelley E. Taylor et al., "Biobehavioral Responses to Stress in Females: Tend-and-Befriend, Not Fight-or-Flight," *Psychological Review* 107, no. 3 (2000): 411–429, https://doi.org/10.1037/0033-295x.107.3.411.

5. University of Rochester Medical Center: Health Encyclopedia, "Stress Can Increase Your Risk for Heart Disease," accessed October 29, 2023, https://www.urmc.rochester .edu/encyclopedia/content.aspxContentTypeID=1&ContentID=2171#:~:text=The%20 hormone%20cortisol%20is%20released,risk%20factors%20for%20heart%20disease.

6. Sami Ouanes and Julius Popp, "High Cortisol and the Risk of Dementia and Alzheimer's Disease: A Review of the Literature," *Frontiers in Aging Neuroscience* 11 (March 1, 2019), https://doi.org/10.3389/fnagi.2019.00043.

7. Jeffrey A. Hall, "Same-Sex Friendships," in *The International Encyclopedia of Interpersonal Communication*, ed. Charles R. Berger and Michael E. Roloff (Malden, MA: Wiley-Blackwell, 2016), https://www.researchgate.net/profile/Jeffrey-Hall-5/publication /314826577_Same-Sex_Friendships/links/5e53e6504585158f40ea0c87/Same-Sex -Friendships.pdf.

8. Yang Yang, Nitesh V. Chawla, and Brian Uzzi, "A Network's Gender Composition and Communication Pattern Predict Women's Leadership Success," *Proceedings of the National Academy of Sciences* 116, no. 6 (2019): 2033–2038, https://doi.org/10.1073 /pnas.1721438116.

9. Society for Research in Child Development, "Teens' Same-Gender Friendships Key to Later Satisfaction in Romantic Relationships," ScienceDaily. January 24, 2019, https:// www.sciencedaily.com/releases/2019/01/190124084924.htm.

10. Kara Alise Christensen et al., "Evaluating Interactions Between Emotion Regulation Strategies Through the Interpersonal Context of Female Friends," *Journal of Clinical Psychology* 78, no. 2 (2012): 266–282, https://doi.org/10.1002/jclp.23214.

11. Robin Dunbar, *Friends: Understanding the Power of Our Most Important Relationships* (Banbury, Oxfordshire, UK: Little, Brown UK, 2021).

12. Marilyn Yalom and Theresa Donovan Brown, *The Social Sex: A History of Female Friendship* (New York: Harper Perennial, 2015).

13. Shena Lashey, *Black Girls Heal*, podcast, May 2, 2023, https://www.blackgirlsheal.org/podcast.

14. Deborah Tannen, *You Just Don't Understand* (London: Virago Press, 1992).

15. Joyce F. Benenson, *Warriors and Worriers: The Survival of the Sexes* (New York: Oxford University Press, 2014).

16. "Feminist Friendship | Dr. Cori Wong | TEDxCSU," YouTube, 2017, video, https://www.youtube.com/watch?v=T9175vYkCSM.

17. Jennifer Lacewell, "The Influence of Perceived Similarity, Affect and Trust on the Performance of Student Learning Groups," *All Graduate Theses, Dissertations, and Other Capstone Projects*, January 2015, https://cornerstone.lib.mnsu.edu/etds/428/.

18. Eiluned Pearce, Anna Machin, and Robin I. M. Dunbar, "Sex Differences in Intimacy Levels in Best Friendships and Romantic Partnerships," *Adaptive Human Behavior and Physiology* (October 2020), https://doi.org/10.1007/s40750-020-00155-z.

19. Deborah Tannen, "The Dynamics of Closeness/Distance and Sameness/Difference in Discourse About Sisters," in *Language in Life, and a Life in Language: Jacob Mey, a Festschrift*, ed. Ken Turner and Bruce Fraser, vol. 6 (Bingley, Bradford, UK: Emerald Group Publishing, 2009).

20. Jaimie Arona Krems et al., "Friendship Jealousy: One Tool for Maintaining Friendships in the Face of Third-Party Threats?" *Journal of Personality and Social Psychology* 120, no. 4 (August 10, 2020), https://doi.org/10.1037/pspi0000311.

21. Keelah E. G. Williams et al., "Sex Differences in Friendship Preferences," *Evolution and Human Behavior* 43, no. 1 (2021), https://doi.org/10.1016/j.evolhumbehav.2021.09.003.

22. J. F. Benenson and A. Christakos, "The Greater Fragility of Females' Versus Males' Closest Same-Sex Friendships," *Child Development* 74 (2003): 1123–1129, https://doi.org/10.1111/1467-8624.00596

23. Joyce Benenson and Richard Wrangham, "Cross-Cultural Sex Differences in Post-Conflict Affiliation Following Sports Matches," *Cell Press* 26, no. 16 (2016), https://doi.org/10.1016/j.cub.2016.06.024.

24. Jeffrey A. Hall, "Sex Differences in Friendship Expectations: A Meta-analysis," *Journal of Social and Personal Relationships* 28, no. 6 (2010): 723–747, https://doi.org/10.1177/0265407510386192.

25. Joyce F. Benenson, *Warriors and Worriers: The Survival of the Sexes* (New York: Oxford University Press, 2014).

26. Shoba Sreenivasan and Linda E. Weinberger, "Conflict in Relationships," *Psychology Today*, 2018, https://www.psychologytoday.com/us/blog/emotional-nourishment/201803/conflict-in-relationships.

27. Harriet Goldhor Lerner, *The Dance of Intimacy: A Woman's Guide to Courageous Acts of Change in Key Relationships* (New York: HarperPerennial, 1990).

28. Eiluned Pearce, Anna Machin, and Robin I. M. Dunbar, "Sex Differences in Intimacy Levels in Best Friendships and Romantic Partnerships," *Adaptive Human Behavior and Physiology* (October 2020), https://doi.org/10.1007/s40750-020-00155-z.

29. Daniel P. Johnson and Mark A. Whisman, "Gender Differences in Rumination: A Meta-analysis," *Personality and Individual Differences* 55, no. 4 (2013): 367–374, https://doi.org/10.1016/j.paid.2013.03.019.

30. Robin Dunbar, *Friends: Understanding the Power of Our Most Important Relationships* (Banbury, Oxfordshire, UK: Little, Brown UK, 2021).

31. Courtney Ricciardi, Olga Kornienko, and Pamela W. Garner, "The Role of Cognitive Emotion Regulation for Making and Keeping Friend and Conflict Networks," *Frontiers in Psychology* 13 (April 2022), https://doi.org/10.3389/fpsyg.2022.802629.

32. John Howard, *More Than Words* (New York: Simon and Schuster/Simon Element, 2023).

33. Bruce Grierson, "Certainty Is a Psychological Trap and It's Time to Escape," *Psychology Today*, July 5, 2023, https://www.psychologytoday.com/us/articles/202307/certainty-is-a-psychological-trap-and-its-time-to-escape.

34. Julia A., Minson, Frances S. Chen, and Catherine H. Tinsley, "Why Won't You Listen to Me? Measuring Receptiveness to Opposing Views," *Management Science* 66, no. 7 (2020): 3069–3094, https://doi.org/10.1287/mnsc.2019.3362.

35. Anne Campbell, *Men, Women and Aggression* (London: British Association Promoting Science and Technology, 1996).

36. Kelly Yu-Hsin Liao, Meifen Wei, and Mengxi Yin, "The Misunderstood Schema of the Strong Black Woman: Exploring Its Mental Health Consequences and Coping Responses Among African American Women," *Psychology of Women Quarterly* 44, no. 1 (2019): 84–104, https://doi.org/10.1177/0361684319883198.

37. Leonardo Christov-Moore et al., "Empathy: Gender Effects in Brain and Behavior," *Neuroscience & Biobehavioral Reviews* 46, no. 4 (2014): 604–627, https://doi.org/10.1016/j.neubiorev.2014.09.001.

38. Tracy Packiam Alloway, *Think Like a Girl: 10 Unique Strengths of a Woman's Brain and How to Make Them Work for You* (Grand Rapids, MI: Zondervan Thrive, 2021).

39. Julia Bear, Laurie R. Weingart, and Gergana Todorova, "Can Avoiding Conflict Be Beneficial? A Field Investigation of Gender, Conflict Avoidance, Emotional Labor, and Emotional Exhaustion," IACM 2011 Istanbul Conference Paper, 2011, *SSRN Electronic Journal*, https://doi.org/10.2139/ssrn.1866524.

40. David Bradford and Carole Robin, *Connect: Building Exceptional Relationships with Family, Friends, and Colleagues* (New York: Currency, 2021).

41. Jillian J. Jordan and Maryam Kouchaki, "Virtuous Victims," *Science Advances* 7, no. 42 (2021), https://www.science.org/doi/10.1126/sciadv.abg5902.

42. Wenjun Yu, "Disrupted Physical Pain Sensation by Social Exclusion in Women with Dysmenorrhea," *Journal of Pain Research* 11 (August 2018): 1469–1477, https://doi.org/10.2147/jpr.s168516.

43. N. I. Eisenberger, "Does Rejection Hurt? An FMRI Study of Social Exclusion," *Science* 302, no. 5643 (2003): 290–292, https://doi.org/10.1126/science.1089134.

44. Joyce F. Benenson et al., "Social Exclusion: More Important to Human Females Than Males," ed. Corrado Sinigagli, *PLoS ONE* 8, no. 2 (2013): e55851, https://doi.org/10.1371/journal.pone.0055851.

45. Radek Ptacek et al., "Clinical Implications of the Perception of Time in Attention Deficit Hyperactivity Disorder (ADHD): A Review," *Medical Science Monitor* 25, no. 25 (2019): 3918–3924, https://doi.org/10.12659/msm.914225.

46. Robert B. Cialdini, *Pre-Suasion: A Revolutionary Way to Influence and Persuade* (New York: Simon & Schuster Paperbacks, 2016).

47. Joan Williams and Marina Multhaup, "For Women and Minorities to Get Ahead, Managers Must Assign Work Fairly," *Harvard Business Review*, May 4, 2018, https://hbr.org/2018/03/for-women-and-minorities-to-get-ahead-managers-must-assign-work-fairly.

48. Azeen Ghorayshi, "More Girls Are Being Diagnosed with Autism," *New York Times*, April 10, 2023, https://www.nytimes.com/2023/04/10/science/autism-rate-girls.html.

49. Elizabeth Vaquera and Grace Kao, "Do You Like Me as Much as I Like You? Friendship Reciprocity and Its Effects on School Outcomes Among Adolescents," *Social Science Research* 37, no. 1 (2008): 55–72, https://doi.org/10.1016/j.ssresearch.2006.11.002.

50. Silvia Federici, "How the Demonization of 'Gossip' Is Used to Break Women's Solidarity," In These Times, January 31, 2019, https://inthesetimes.com/article/the-subversive-feminist-power-of-gossip.

51. Jennifer K. Bosson et al., "Interpersonal Chemistry Through Negativity: Bonding by Sharing Negative Attitudes About Others," *Personal Relationships* 13, no. 2 (2006): 135–150, https://doi.org/10.1111/j.1475-6811.2006.00109.x.

52. Francesca Giardini and Rafael Wittek, "Gossip, Reputation, and Sustainable Cooperation," in *The Oxford Handbook of Gossip and Reputation* (New York: Oxford University Press, 2019), https://www.rafaelwittek.eu/images/Giardini_Wittek_2019_Gossip_Reputation_and_Sustainable_Cooperation_Sociological_Foundations_Online.pdf.

53. Jennifer Coates, *Women, Men and Language: A Sociolinguistic Account of Gender Differences in Language* (Abingdon, Oxfordshire, UK: Routledge, 2016).

54. Kerry Cohen, *Crazy for You: Breaking the Spell of Sex and Love Addiction* (New York: Hachette Go, 2021).

55. Kaila Yu, "How to Spot a Love Addict," *New York Times*, September 23, 2021, https://www.nytimes.com/2021/09/23/well/love-addiction-sex-toxic-relationships.html.

56. "Any Anxiety Disorder," National Institute of Mental Health, 2017, https://www.nimh.nih.gov/health/statistics/any-anxiety-disorder.

57. Barbara Neal Varma, "Complaining, for Your Health," *Atlantic*, February 8, 2015, https://www.theatlantic.com/health/archive/2015/02/complaining-for-your-health/385041/.

58. Robin M. Kowalski et al., "Pet Peeves and Happiness: How Do Happy People Complain?" *Journal of Social Psychology* 154 no. 4 (2014): 278–282, https://doi.org/10.1080/00224545.2014.906380.

59. Veronika Engert et al., "Cortisol Increase in Empathic Stress Is Modulated by Emotional Closeness and Observation Modality," *Psychoneuroendocrinology*, no. 45 (July 2014): 192–201, https://doi.org/10.1016/j.psyneuen.2014.04.005.

60. Elaine Fawcett, "Effects of Complaining Versus Gratitude on Brain Health," NeuroLife, May 14, 2018, https://www.neurolifecenter.com/2018/05/14/effects-of-complaining-versus-gratitude-on-brain-health/#:~:text=Chronic%20complaining%20results%20from%20a.

61. Kyle Benson, "The Magic Relationship Ratio, According to Science," Gottman Institute, October 4, 2017, https://www.gottman.com/blog/the-magic-relationship-ratio-according-science/.

62. Joel Bahr, "Gratitude Is Good—Even If It Doesn't Always Feel Like It," University of California, November 20, 2018, https://www.universityofcalifornia.edu/news/gratitude-good-even-if-it-doesnt-always-feel-it#:~:text=%E2%80%9CThere%20is%20a%20whole%20range.

63. Suzanne Degges-White, "The 13 Essential Traits of Good Friends," *Psychology Today*, March 23, 2015, https://www.psychologytoday.com/us/blog/lifetime-connections/201503/the-13-essential-traits-good-friends.

64. Julianne Holt-Lunstad et al., "On the Importance of Relationship Quality: The Impact of Ambivalence in Friendships on Cardiovascular Functioning," *Annals of Behavioral Medicine* 33, no. 3 (2007): 278–290, https://doi.org/10.1007/bf02879910.

65. Molly McPherson, *Indestructible: Reclaim Control and Respond with Confidence in a Media Crisis* (Mandala Tree Press, 2021).

66. Jamie Ballard, "Two-Thirds of Americans Say They've Ended a Friendship," YouGov, May 8, 2023, https://today.yougov.com/topics/society/articles-reports/2023/05/08/americans-ended-friendship-breakups-poll.

67. Gary W. Lewandowski, "Promoting Positive Emotions Following Relationship Dissolution Through Writing," *Journal of Positive Psychology* 4, no. 1 (2009): 21–31, https://doi.org/10.1080/17439760802068480.

68. Lewandowski, "Promoting Positive Emotions."

69. Kobe Campbell, *Why Am I Like This?: How to Break Cycles, Heal Your Trauma, and Restore Your Faith* (Nashville: Thomas Nelson, 2023).

70. Robin Dunbar, *Friends: Understanding the Power of Our Most Important Relationships* (Banbury, Oxfordshire, UK: Little, Brown UK, 2021).

71. Kunal Bhattacharya et al., "Sex Differences in Social Focus Across the Life Cycle in Humans." *Royal Society Open Science* 3, no. 4 (2016), https://doi.org/10.1098/rsos.160097.

72. Lois M. Verbrugge, "Multiplexity in Adult Friendships," *Social Forces* 57, no. 4 (1979): 1286, https://doi.org/10.2307/2577271.

73. Peggy Liu, "The Surprise of Reaching Out: Appreciated More Than We Think," *SSRN Electronic Journal*, 2022, https://doi.org/10.2139/ssrn.4115683.

74. Nicholas Epley, *Mindwise: How We Misunderstand What Others Think, Believe, Feel, and Want* (New York: Vintage Books, 2015).

75. David Bradford and Carole Robin, *Connect: Building Exceptional Relationships with Family, Friends, and Colleagues* (New York: Currency, 2021).

76. Sheon Han, "You Can Only Maintain so Many Close Friendships," *The Atlantic*, May 20, 2021, https://www.theatlantic.com/family/archive/2021/05/robin-dunbar-explains-circles-friendship-dunbars-number/618931/.

77. Jill Suttie, "How to Keep Connecting with Strangers During the Pandemic," Greater Good, October 6, 2020, https://greatergood.berkeley.edu/article/item/how_to_keep_connecting_with_strangers_during_the_pandemic.

78. Laura Tremaine, *The Life Council* (Nashville: Zondervan, 2023).

79. N. E. Newall et al., "Causal Beliefs, Social Participation, and Loneliness Among Older Adults: A Longitudinal Study," *Journal of Social and Personal Relationships* 26, nos. 2–3 (2009), 273–290, https://doi.org/10.1177/0265407509106718.

80. Tracy Brower, "New Study: Making Friends Is Hard but Work Can Help," Forbes, October 5, 2022, https://www.forbes.com/sites/tracybrower/2022/10/05/new-study-making-friends-is-hard-but-work-can-help/?sh=1aeae7a67a77.

81. Marisa G. Franco, *Platonic: How the Science of Attachment Can Help You Make—and Keep—Friends* (New York: Putnam, 2022).

82. Sanaz Talaifar and William B. Swann, "Self-Verification Theory," *Encyclopedia of Personality and Individual Differences*, no. 17 (January 2017): 1–9, https://doi.org/10.1007/978-3-319-28099-8_1180-1.

83. Gili Freedman et al., "Ghosting and Destiny: Implicit Theories of Relationships Predict Beliefs About Ghosting," *Journal of Social and Personal Relationships* 36, no. 3 (2018): 905–924, https://doi.org/10.1177/0265407517748791.

84. Nathaniel M. Lambert et al., "The Role of Appreciation in Close Relationships: A Journal Study," 2008, https://diginole.lib.fsu.edu/islandora/object/fsu:181628/datastream/PDF/view.

Index